STARTING YOUR NEW BUSINESS:

A Guide for Entrepreneurs

Revised Edition

Charles L. Martin

A FIFTY-MINUTE™ SERIES BOOK

CRISP PUBLICATIONS, INC.
Menlo Park, California

STARTING YOUR NEW BUSINESS
A Guide For Entrepreneurs
Revised Edition

Charles L. Martin

CREDITS
Editor: **Michael Crisp**
Layout and Composition: **Interface Studio**
Cover Design: **Carol Harris**
Artwork: **Ralph Mapson**
Research Assistance: **Priscilla Hathaway and Mark O'Neill**

Copyright © 1992 by Crisp Publications, Inc.
Printed in the United States of America

English language Crisp books are distributed worldwide. Our major international distributors include:

CANADA: Reid Publishing Ltd., Box 69559—109 Thomas St., Oakville, Ontario, Canada L6J 7R4. TEL: (905) 842-4428, FAX: (905) 842-9327

Raincoast Books Distribution Ltd., 112 East 3rd Avenue, Vancouver, British Columbia, Canada V5T 1C8. TEL: (604) 873-6581, FAX: (604) 874-2711

AUSTRALIA: Career Builders, P.O. Box 1051, Springwood, Brisbane, Queensland, Australia 4127. TEL: 841-1061, FAX: 841-1580

NEW ZEALAND: Career Builders, P.O. Box 571, Manurewa, Auckland, New Zealand. TEL: 266-5276, FAX: 266-4152

JAPAN: Phoenix Associates Co., Mizuho Bldg. 2-12-2, Kami Osaki, Shinagawa-Ku, Tokyo 141, Japan. TEL: 3-443-7231, FAX: 3-443-7640

Selected Crisp titles are also available in other languages. Contact International Rights Manager Suzanne Kelly at (415) 323-6100 for more information.

Library of Congress Catalog Card Number 91-77079
Martin, Charles L.
Starting Your New Business, Revised Edition
ISBN 1-56052-144-9

This book is printed on recyclable paper with soy ink.

ABOUT THIS BOOK

STARTING YOUR NEW BUSINESS is not like most books. It has a unique "self-paced" format that encourages a reader to become personally involved. Designed to be "read with a pencil," there are an abundance of exercises, activities, and assessments and cases that invite participation.

The objective of this book is to help a reader think through all of the critical issues before charging ahead to set up a new business. It contains several hundred questions that, if answered honestly, will assist with a decision of whether or not to start a business.

For readers already familiar with the first edition, you should note several changes in the revised edition, facts, statistics, and examples have been updated and several new discussions added. They include: 1) Women in Entrepreneurship, 2) Product Quality, 3) Franchising, and 4) Business Exit Planning, to name a few.

This book is part of a series of similar self-help books. For more information on other titles that are available, please turn to the back of this book.

— Individual Study. Because the book is self-instructional, all that is needed is a quiet place, some time and a pencil. By completing the activities and exercises, a person should not only receive valuable feedback, but also practical ideas about steps for self-improvement.

— Workshops and Seminars. The book is ideal for pre-assigned reading prior to a workshop or seminar. With the basics in hand, the quality of the participation should improve. More time can be spent on concept extensions and applications during the program. The book can also be effective when a trainer distributes it at the beginning of a session, and leads participants through the contents.

— Remote Location Training. Copies can be sent to those not able to attend "home office" training sessions.

— Informal Study Groups. Thanks to the format, brevity and low cost, this book is ideal for "brown-bag" or other informal group sessions.

There are other possibilities that depend on the objectives, program or ideas or the user. One thing for sure, even after it has been read, this book will serve as excellent reference material which can be easily reviewed.

PREFACE

So, you've been thinking about starting your own business? Perhaps you've had a great idea for some time and finally mustered the courage to see what it takes to start a small business. Perhaps you mowed lawns or baby-sat as a youngster and miss those days of independence and autonomy. Perhaps you're having trouble making ends meet and think that operating a business in your spare time may be the answer.

Whatever your motivations are for wanting to start a new business, this book can help you. But it is essential that you understand what this book is and what it is not.

This book is...	**This book is *not*...**
• A good place to start. It will give you a ''feel'' for what is involved in being an entrepreneur.	• The only source of information you'll need. No single book can accomplish everything you'll need to know.
• Realistic. It is based upon solid business wisdom presented in a straightforward and objective manner.	• A get-rich-quick scheme. Owning and operating a small business requires *hard* work and *smart* work. No illusions to the contrary are fostered.
• A resource that asks almost one thousand questions. If you don't know which questions to ask in business, you'll probably never find the answers you need.	• A book of almost a thousand answers, because no two businesses are alike. Some answers are included, but the primary objective is to point you in the right direction so you can find answers for your specific business.

To make the best use of this book, first read it casually—from cover to cover. Such a reading will give you an overview of what is involved in starting and owning a small business. Then read it again, carefully—with a pencil and plenty of note paper. Try to answer the questions as you go, work the exercises and take notes. Follow-up by using some of the recommended techniques as well as items listed in the ''Additional Sources'' section. If you'll follow these suggestions, the chances of your new business being a successful one will increase greatly.

Good Luck!

Charles L. Martin

Charles L. Martin

CONTENTS

PART ONE

THE NATURE OF ENTREPRENEURSHIP AND ENTREPRENEURS

"It is easy to find fault with a new idea.
It is easier to say it can't be done, than to try.
Thus, it is through the fear of failure,
That some men create their own Hell."

E. Jacob Taylor

THE NATURE OF ENTREPRENEURSHIP

Part of the American dream is to someday own your own business. For most of us, this dream is within reach. Opportunities for owning and operating small businesses abound. About 675,000 businesses are started each year and most are founded by people probably not unlike yourself. There are currently more than 17 million small, non-farm businesses in the U.S., but by the year 2000, this number is expected to grow to 25 million. That's 25 million separate entities that began with an entrepreneur's dream and desire to succeed.

To a budding entrepreneur, starting a small business offers the opportunity for a personally and financially rewarding endeavor—a chance to ''battle the world,'' to build something from scratch, to control one's destiny, to be independent and work autonomously, to satisfy a genuine need in the community, to grow as an individual, and to have no one else limit the business' horizons.

The Facts of Small Business In The U.S.

- 87% of all businesses employ less than 20 employees.

- More than 27% of all workers work in businesses that employ less than 20 employees and 56% of the labor force work in businesses employing fewer than 100 employees.

- The size of the ''average'' business is decreasing: The number of businesses is growing faster than the Gross National Product.

- Entrepreneurs are innovative: Patents issued to individuals are on the rise—jumping 37% from 1986 to 1990.

- Small businesses access world markets: 60% of firms who successfully export abroad are small businesses employing fewer than 100 workers.

- About 70% of the small businesses started this year are predicted to fail within five years.

- Despite the failures, the number of small businesses is expected to grow by more than 40% in the 1990s.

- In the late 1970s, about one thousand college students were enrolled in entrepreneurship courses. Today, several hundred colleges and universities offer entrepreneurship courses for thousands of students.

THE NATURE OF ENTREPRENEURSHIP (Continued)

The glamorous and exciting lure of starting a small business blinds many to the stark realities of entrepreneurship. The risks and disadvantages should not be quietly dismissed because they are very real. For example, 55,000 to 65,000 small businesses fail each year. Many of these failing businesses take with them the life savings (and often the self-esteem) of their founders. If past trends continue, about 70% of all small businesses started this year will fail by their fifth year. Of those 30% that somehow manage to survive, many will not be as financially rewarding as originally envisioned.

Beyond the financial risk of insolvency, there are numerous personal drawbacks facing those who start their own business. Successful small business owners, for example, rarely enjoy the luxury of a standard work day. As an owner of a small retail clothing store explained, ''Owning your own business means working Saturdays forever.'' The responsibility of running the business ultimately lies with the proprietor, a role that can be stressful and lonely. The most difficult decisions and unpleasant tasks cannot be delegated. Also, most small business owners find they are not as independent as they initially believed. Customers, suppliers, and government agencies become the proprietor's new ''bosses'' and they are equally (if not more) demanding than any boss in a ''big business''.

Some owners grow to hate their businesses and/or their partners. They may feel trapped—unable to sell the business or dissolve the partnership as quickly as they'd like. So, as you see, starting a business is not something to be undertaken casually or lightly.

Clearly, there are opportunities for successful small business ventures, but anyone considering going into business for himself or herself is well-advised to weigh the pros and cons. In other words, look before you leap!

Beating the Odds

Because you are continuing to read, you must still be interested in starting a business. Either you didn't read carefully, or else the advantages and promise of small business ownership outweighed the disadvantages and risks described. If this is the case, the question becomes: What does it take to beat the odds and enhance the likelihood for a successful business venture? What do profitable, on-going, businesses have in common? Take a moment and list as many success factors as you can in the space provided.

SMALL BUSINESS SUCCESS FACTORS

1. _____

2. _____

3. _____

4. _____

5. _____

6. _____

7. _____

8. _____

THE NATURE OF
ENTREPRENEURSHIP (Continued)

If the factors you listed on page 3 are consistent with small business experts, at least one success factor focused on the **personal characteristics** of the entrepreneur: a person who is independent, not afraid of working hard, with a high need of power and/or achievement, who enjoys good health, and so on. Another success factor you may have listed is **prior experience** as an entrepreneur or expertise in a particular industry. Every type of business has its own "ins and outs," its own idiosyncrasies. And experience is the best teacher when it comes to learning a specific industry or type of operation. Your list should have included a **winning idea**. Winning ideas are not only superior to competitors' offerings, but are also in demand by your potential customers. There is no such thing as a better mousetrap if consumers are completely satisfied with the mousetraps they've purchased for years. Another key factor is that every successful business venture must have **a plan**—a blue print, to safely guide the business toward its objectives. Finally successful businesses must have **sufficient funds** to not only open the doors, but to keep them open for several months during the slow and expensive start-up period. If you listed most of these success factors, congratulations! All of them will be discussed in greater detail throughout this book.

Another way of beating the odds is to understand some of the major pitfalls that so often lead to business failure. The facing page summarizes several pitfalls and suggests ways to avoid them.

PITFALLS OF OPERATING YOUR OWN BUSINESS

Pitfalls

1. Lack of Experience
2. Lack of Money/Capital
3. The Wrong Location
4. Inventory Mismanagement
5. Too Much Capital Going Into Fixed Assets
6. Poor Credit Granting Practices
7. Taking Too Much Personal Income
8. Failing to Plan
9. Having the Wrong Attitude
10. Choosing the Wrong Partners
11. Not Knowing Yourself
12. Having Unrealistic Expectations

What Can Be Done About These Pitfalls?

1. Recognize Limitations
2. Plan Properly
3. Keep Records
4. Watch the Balance Sheet—Not Just the Profits
5. Investigate
6. Cooperate With Suppliers and Banks
7. Learn
8. Utilize Professional Assistance
9. Watch Your Health

Sources: *The Pitfalls in Managing a Small Business*, W.H. Kuehn, New York: Dun and Bradstreet, 1973 and *"Classic Causes of Entrepreneurial Failure,"* Roger H. Ford, *Business Perspectives*, Spring 1989, pp.22-23.

DO YOU HAVE WHAT IT TAKES?

> "Real opportunities lie within a person, not outside.
> What lies behind you and what lies before you are
> tiny matters compared to what lies within you."
> Ralph Waldo Emerson

As shown below, entrepreneurs have backgrounds as varied as the nature of their ventures. Many start their businesses as youngsters in their twenties, while others wait until retirement from a career. Formal education seems to be a "plus," but is not absolutely essential. Most entrepreneurs in the past have been male, but females are making substantial inroads in small business ownership.

BACKGROUNDS OF ENTREPRENEURS

- Twenty-five percent started their business before age 30. Eleven percent were over age 50 when they started theirs.

- Thirty-two percent graduated from high school but never attended college. Twenty-seven percent earned a Bachelors and/or an advanced college degree.

- Forty-five percent have parents who owned an independent business. Forty-six percent had been previously employed in a small business.

- The percentage of minorities in the U.S. who own their own businesses is increasing with these groups leading the way: Korean (10.2%), Asian Indian (7.6%), Japanese (6.6%), Chinese (6.3%), Cuban (6.3%), and Vietnamese (4.9%). Women too are making great strides in entrepreneurship as shown in the next box.

For Women Only

- About 30% of the nation's businesses are women-owned, accounting for almost $280 billion in revenues.

- The number of women who own small businesses in the U.S. is increasing at a rate four times faster than that of men.

- Most firms owned by women are less than five years old and have four or fewer workers.

- Female entrepreneurs tend to start their businesses about a decade later than male entrepreneurs—usually between the ages of 35 and 45.

- Businesses in retailing, insurance, and real estate are popular ventures started by a high proportion of women.

WHAT MAKES A SUCCESSFUL ENTREPRENEUR?

More reliable predictors of successful entrepreneurs involve the assessment of each individual's aptitudes and level of motivation. Many schools and some government agencies provide testing services to help prospective entrepreneurs to diagnose their strengths and weaknesses. One such program is called GATB— General Aptitude Tests Battery.

If you can be objective, a self-assessment of your entrepreneurial potential may be a viable alternative to formal tests such as GATB. Robert Schaefer in his manual *Starting and Managing a Small Service Business** recommends that a self-assessment should begin with your honest answer to the following question:

> Knowing what I do about myself, would I hire someone like me to run a business that I have invested my life savings in?

If your answer to the above question was yes, you should next list your work experience, skills, and education much like an employment agency might ask you to do. Such a list will help you to identify your weaknesses that might be strengthened with additional preparation.

The Small Business Administration provides a structured self-assessment questionnaire (reproduced on the next page) that will help you learn if you've got what it takes to be an entrepreneur. Check the answer under each question that best reflects the way you honestly feel. After you have answered all of the questions, read the instructions for interpreting your self-assessment.

ASSESSMENT AHEAD

*Source: *Starting and Managing a Small Service Business*, Robert A. Schaefer, Washington D.C.: U.S. Small Business Administration, 1986, page 8.

CHECKLIST FOR GOING INTO BUSINESS

Are you a self-starter?

____ I do things on my own. Nobody has to tell me to get going.

____ If someone gets me started I keep going all right.

____ Easy does it. I don't put myself out until I have to.

How do you feel about other people?

____ I like people. I can get along with just about anybody.

____ I have plenty of friends—I don't need anyone else.

____ Most people irritate me.

Can you lead others?

____ I can get most people to go along when I start doing something.

____ I can give orders if someone tells me what we should do.

____ I let someone else get things moving. Then I go along if I feel like it.

Can you take responsibility?

____ I like to take charge of things and see them through.

____ I'll take over if I have to, but I'd rather let someone else be responsible.

____ There is always some eager beaver around wanting to show how smart he is. I say let him.

How good an organizer are you?

____ I like to have a plan before I start. I'm usually the one to get things lined up when the group wants to do something.

____ I do all right unless things get too confused. Then I quit.

____ You get all set and then something comes along and presents too many problems. So I just take things as they come.

How good a worker are you?

____ I can keep going as long as I need to. I don't mind working hard for something I want.

____ I'll work hard for a while, but when I've had enough, that's it.

____ I can't see that hard work gets you anywhere.

Can you make decisions?

____ I can make up my mind in a hurry if I have to. It usually turns out O.K., too.

____ I can if I have plenty of time. If I have to make up my mind fast, I think later I should have decided the other way.

____ I don't like to be the one who has to decide things.

Can people trust what you say?

____ You bet they can. I don't say things I don't mean.

____ I try to be on the level most of the time, but sometimes I just say what's easiest.

____ Why bother if the other fellow doesn't know the difference.

Can you stick with it?

____ If I make up my mind to do something, I don't let anything stop me.

____ I usually finish what I start—if it goes well.

____ If it doesn't go right away, I quit. Why beat your brains out?

How good is your health?

____ I never run down!

____ I have enough energy for most things I want to do.

____ I seem to run out of energy sooner than most of my friends seem to.

Source: *Checklist for Going Into Business*, Management Aid #2.016, U.S. Small Business Administration, 1985.

INTERPRETING THE SELF-ASSESSMENT QUESTIONNAIRE

Are most of your checks beside the first response choices? If so, congratulations! You've probably got what it takes to own and operate a business. If many of your checks are beside the second choices, consider teaming-up with a partner who can offset your weaker areas. If you've checked many of the third responses, you might pat yourself on the back for being honest and then seriously consider working for someone else.

TEN INGREDIENTS FOR SUCCESS

Here are ten ingredients James R. Paul, CEO for Coastal Corporation, says it takes to be a successful entrepreneur. Can you identify with these characteristics? Do you have what it takes?

1. Hard work: plain, old-fashioned hard work.

2. Focus: you must be able to concentrate on what you do best.

3. Good ideas: look for good ideas like a dog looks for a fire plug. Everyday look for new ideas, new methods, new ways to improve, to grow—new ways to raise productivity, to find new customers, to control costs, and to eliminate bureaucracy.

4. Flexibility: flexibility succeeds.

5. Adaptability to change: adapt to change, but also learn to anticipate it.

6. Sales: you must be able to get others to buy into your idea.

7. Confidence: all successful people simply ooze confidence from every pore.

8. Balance: between detail and general thinking. A sense of perspective is important.

9. Assertiveness: all successful people use it to their advantage.

10. Improvement: constantly improve yourself and your company.

Source: Speech by James R. Paul, March 27, 1991, Wichita, Kansas: Wichita State University, Center for Entrepreneurship.

PART TWO

DOING YOUR HOMEWORK

If, after reading Part One, you're still convinced you'd like to become an entrepreneur, we hope you are also convinced that business isn't something to be entered casually. To become successful, you've *first* got to do your homework. Homework involves a preliminary screening and analysis of your business ideas, preparation of a business plan, and securing the capital you need to get started.

SCREENING YOUR BUSINESS IDEAS

Most small business ventures begin with the identification of a key idea or concept. Eventually the concept is parlayed into some core products or services that, ideally, offer unique benefits and advantages over the competition. The majority of these ideas come from previous work experience, or personal interest. Other ideas can originate from the suggestions of friends, educational training or simply being in the right place at the right time.

A major pitfall to avoid is to become so enthusiastic for the idea that it prevents *objectively* evaluating the idea's potential. It is easy to fall into such a trap especially when your own idea is at stake. That's why many corporations may initially screen a dozen or more ideas for each one new product they introduce.

To help you better screen your business ideas consider the following three considerations.

1

Generate a number of new product/service ideas. Reflect upon prior experiences and personal interest for new ideas, but also brainstorm with friends and family. Read, read, and read some more, staying alert to trends in business and society that may give rise to new business opportunities.

2

Ask yourself tough questions about each idea. These questions will help you weed out losing ideas before you commit additional time and resources. Following are examples of questions you can use to screen most new product/service ideas. If you can't answer these questions, you probably need to investigate further.

QUESTION:	YES	MAYBE	NO	NOT RELEVANT
• Is there a genuine need for the product?*	——	——	——	——
• Is the need substantial enough to support a profitable business?	——	——	——	——
• Do competitors currently offer similar products? If ''yes'', does your idea offer distinctive advantages and customer benefits the competitors' don't?	——	——	——	——
• Is the product feasible to produce?	——	——	——	——
• Is the product legal?	——	——	——	——
• Is it safe?	——	——	——	——
• If the product is a durable good, can it be easily serviced? (Also, *who* will service it?)	——	——	——	——
• Are the investment costs required to develop, produce, and market the product reasonable, within your financial realities?	——	——	——	——
• Is the ''pay-back period'' fast enough to allow you to stay in business?	——	——	——	——
• Can the product be expanded into a line of similar or compatible items later, if the original was successful?	——	——	——	——
• Can you protect the product with a patent or copyright?	——	——	——	——
• Does the product infringe upon anyone else's patents or copyrights?	——	——	——	——
• Are the needed raw materials and supplies readily available?	——	——	——	——

Starting Your New Business: A Guide For Entrepreneurs

---

*Note: ''Product'' is a generic term used throughout this book to refer to tangible goods, services, or some combination.

SCREENING YOUR BUSINESS IDEAS
(Continued)

Conduct some exploratory research to test the waters. Many entrepreneurs have failed because they could not confidently answer the questions in Step 2. Others failed because they were so convinced of the soundness of their business idea they completely bypassed the opinions and reactions of industry experts, such as: suppliers, middlemen, and most importantly, end users or consumers. In both instances, exploratory research could effectively further screen ideas and increase the likelihood of selecting ideas with the greatest potential.

Following are three popular (and relatively inexpensive) techniques you can use for exploratory research:

- *Literature Surveys and Secondary Data.* (a.k.a. ''rummaging around in the library''). The voluminous nature of reference material and secondary data (e.g. census data) that can be found in the library is spectacular. Books, periodicals, journals, government documents and other sources in the library address the following types of issues for each business idea:

  —Statistical information

    —Characteristics of competitors

    —Industry trends (e.g. revenues)

    —Consumer characteristics (demographic and otherwise)

    —Characteristics of suppliers

  —Qualitative information

    —Identification of industry leaders, experts, or trade associations

    —Identification of potential suppliers

    —Ideas pertaining to the future of the industry

    —Current issues facing the industry

    —Technical ''how to'' information (e.g. how to develop a blueprint to accompany a patent application).

- *Experience Surveys.* This informal technique involves picking the brains of people in the same or similar businesses who hold differing viewpoints and perspectives. If a new product is the core of your business idea, for example, query the following people:

    —Engineers, e.g., Can the product be effectively and efficiently designed?

    —Suppliers, e.g. Are the necessary materials, component parts and manufacturing facilities readily available at a reasonable price?

    —Middlemen, e.g. Would retailers be receptive to carrying your products?

    —Government officials and/or lawyers e.g. Are there any licensing, safety, or environmental requirements of which you should be aware? Will warning labels or disclaimers be required?

    —Competitors, e.g. How are they doing? What changes have they made in product design, pricing, distribution, etc.?

- *Focus Groups.* To solicit initial consumer reactions to your business ideas, conduct a series of informal discussions with small groups of consumers. Properly structured, these focus groups can provide helpful feedback to questions such as those listed below. (Note: be cautious because consumers are often more enthusiastic in a focus group than when faced with an actual purchasing decision):

    —Describe the ''typical'' purchaser.

    —Why might someone *not* be interested in the product?

    —If the product weren't available, would the typical consumer settle for a substitute?

    —How many units would the typical consumer purchase? How frequently? At what price? Who makes the purchasing decision?

    —What is liked and disliked about similar competing products?

    —How should the item be packaged? What color(s) should the product be? What size? What special features (e.g. a handle)?

After the initial screening process is completed, more conclusive research may be necessary to accurately estimate the feasibility of the most promising business idea. This research might include prototype development, formal surveys, test markets, etc. These forms of research can be expensive and should not be undertaken until the business idea has survived the exploratory research stage.

A BUSINESS PLAN: WHAT IT IS AND WHY ONE IS ESSENTIAL

> *"If you don't know where you're going, any path will take you there."*
>
> —*Theodore Levitt*

What Is A Business Plan?

A business plan is a carefully prepared document that outlines the nature of the business, the objectives of the entrepreneur and the proposed actions that will be required to reach those objectives. As such, a business plan is analogous to a roadmap. It should be capable of guiding the entrepreneur through a maze of business decisions and alternatives that successfully avoid sidestreets and dead ends.

Why Plan?

Although not every entrepreneur formally prepares a business plan before starting his or her business, the advantages of doing so far outweigh the disadvantages. For example:

- The process of preparing a plan stimulates thought. This requires the person drafting it to think things through and explicitly articulate and face critical issues that might otherwise be ignored or postponed.

- A comprehensive business plan facilitates a greater coordination and integration of details than would be possible if the business were simply operated on a day-to-day basis.

- A well written plan will help an entrepreneur communicate with others (i.e. partners, employees, or investors) by clearly articulating the vision and expectations of the business.

- A thorough, concise, and persuasive plan will convince lenders and investors that the entrepreneur is serious about starting a business and has done the required homework. This increases the likelihood that the business venture will be adequately funded.

- A written plan serves as a reference document that can be used to measure progress toward business goals, and as a foundation for future planning.

Avoid Excuses

Despite the advantages of preparing a written business plan, some hopeful entrepreneurs bypass the process. Instead they opt to rely on informal, or vague plans that either prevent the start-up or ultimately limit the effectiveness of the business. If you are reluctant to prepare a formal written plan, you may wish to reconsider your position after reading the following "excuses" to avoid doing a plan:

- *Time pressures.* If your excuse is that you don't have the time to prepare a plan, how will you find the time to operate a business after the start-up? Planning done properly doesn't take time; it saves time.

- *Fear of failure.* Planning involves specifying goals and setting objectives. If you are reluctant to commit your goals and objectives to paper where others may see them, maybe you're afraid others will say "I told you so" should you fail. If that's the case, perhaps you're not thick-skinned enough to start your own business. Besides, if you don't articulate your goals, how will you know when you've reached them?

- *Limited understanding of the business, industry, or customer.* Planning is difficult when knowledge is lacking. Goals, strategies and operational decisions become fuzzy and it's impossible to meaningfully commit fuzziness to paper. If your base of knowledge is insufficient, perhaps the initial analysis of your business idea was inadequate. If so, it may be wiser to postpone the preparation of the plan rather than ignoring doing a plan altogether.

- *Poor writing skills.* * Much of a plan's preparation involves sitting at a desk or table and writing, rewriting, and revising the plan. This may be mentally tiring and time consuming for individuals without previous writing experience. Since writing is a basic form of business communication, consider using the plan as an opportunity to polish your writing skills.

- *Low self-confidence.* The preparation of a plan implies that the person preparing it has control over the implementation and accomplishment of the plan. Understandably there may be a reluctance to plan when the would-be planner believes the destiny of the business is randomly determined. Rarely, however, does sheer luck determine the fate of business.

---

*For two excellent books on business writing, order *Better Business Writing* and *Writing Fitness* using the information in the back of this book.

STEPS IN THE PLANNING PROCESS

> *"It's not the writing that's difficult—it's the thinking."*
> *James Leigh*

Before committing a business plan to paper, it is useful to think through the planning process analytically. That is, determine how to gather the data needed, identify factors that could influence the successful implementation of your plan, choose between alternative courses of action, bombard yourself with "what if...?" questions, anticipate results, and formulate contingency strategies. The process involves a continuous sequence of eight interrelated steps as shown below.

EIGHT STEPS TO A BETTER BUSINESS PLAN

STEP #1

Conduct a Situation Analysis.

A situation analysis involves a careful review of the environment in which the business will compete. In other words, what are the potential problems, opportunities, threats, trends, and other issues that are likely to influence the success of the business and the selection of which business strategies to employ? The situation analysis should scrutinize the market in terms of customer characteristics and the nature of the customer-product relationship. A careful evaluation of specific competitors can be quite revealing, as can a comprehensive review of alternative sites where the business might be located. The check lists on the following pages may be used to systematize your analysis. Much of the needed information may have already been collected during your process of screening business ideas.

CUSTOMER/PRODUCT ANALYSIS

Ask the following questions for each major product group and for each major customer segment. But don't *just* ask the questions; find the answers, investigate past trends and likely future trends, and carefully consider the implications.

- Who is the likely customer?
  —Where does s/he live?
  —What is his/her age?
  —What is his/her income?
  —What is his/her level of education?
  —If the likely customers are other businesses...
    —What is their size?
    —What are their normal, expected discounts?
    —Who are their customers?
    —Who normally makes the purchasing decision?
    —What are their purchasing procedures?

- How many potential customers are there?

- What are customers' quality expectations?

- Are customers likely to perceive a purchase risk?

- What needs does the product satisfy (think carefully about this question)?

CONDUCT A SITUATION ANALYSIS
(Continued)

- How is the product used?

- Are there alternative uses?

- Is the product a necessary or discretionary item?

- How many units is the customer likely to buy?

- How often will the customer buy?

- When will the customer buy (day of the week, time of day, season of year, etc.)?

- If the product is a service, does the customer need to be present when the service is provided?

- Where would the customer learn about the product (e.g. friends, business associates, TV advertising, yellow pages, etc.)?

- Who *actually buys* the product (e.g. Mom, Purchasing agent, other)?

- Who *influences the decision* to buy? (e.g. kids, engineers, etc.)?

- Why should the customer buy your product and not the competitor's?

- How much prior knowledge does the customer have about the product (i.e., is it truly a new innovation)?

- How much would the customer likely pay for the product?

- How sensitive would she/he likely be to price changes?

CHECKLIST FOR EVALUATING A LOCATION

Once you've selected a community or neighborhood for your business, use the following questions to evaluate specific sites. The importance of each factor will depend upon the size of your operation, as well as the type of business. For instance, availability of customer parking is usually more critical for retailers than for manufacturers.

✔ What is the total cost for renting or acquiring the property?

✔ What is the estimated cost for any necessary repairs, remodeling, or renovation (What about special heating, lighting, or ventilation requirements)?

✔ Does the site provide as much space as you need...including parking and possible expansion later?

✔ If customers will visit your place of business
   —Is adequate, convenient, and safe parking available?
   —Is public transportation available?
   —Is the location likely to generate drop-in or impulse consumer traffic?
   —Is the site located in a familiar area (e.g., a mall)? If not, will savings in rental or acquisition costs offset the increased costs required to inform and encourage customers to come to your location?

✔ What are the zoning regulations for the site and for the surrounding area?

✔ What other types of businesses are located in the area? Are they compatible with your business?

✔ Are there vacancies in the area? If so, why?

✔ What is the crime rate for the immediate area? Is insurance available? Is it affordable?

✔ What about fire and police protection?

✔ Are adequate utilities available at a reasonable cost (e.g., water, electricity, sewer, gas, etc.)?

CONDUCT A SITUATION ANALYSIS
(Continued)

Checklist (continued)

✔ If snow is a likely problem in the winter, are snow removal services available? Is the site located along a high priority "snow route," or on a side street that may not be plowed at all?

✔ Will you pick up and/or deliver? If so, is the site located near expressways or major arteries to minimize driving time?

✔ If the site is for rent or lease, what are the terms of the rental agreement? Consider length of lease, renewal option, penalties for breaking the lease, services provided by the landlord, maintenance or other fees, etc.

✔ What is the history of the site? That is, what types of businesses previously occupied the site? Why are they no longer there?

For some small businesses, the ideal location may be in a basement, a spare room, or in a closet in the entrepreneur's home. Overhead costs are low, there are often tax advantages, and the daily commute is unbeatable! Research indicates that 56% of entrepreneurs who work out of their homes believe their efforts are more productive than if their businesses were located elsewhere. Not surprisingly, the number of self-employed individuals working at home in the U.S. rose to 11.8 million in 1991—more than a 5% increase from the previous year. If your business isn't the type to jeopardize the residential flavor of the neighborhood by contributing to automobile traffic and conjestion, noise, air pollution, or requiring substantial outside signage or storage, then there's an excellent chance that local authorities will tolerate your home-based business.

ANALYZE YOUR COMPETITION

Use the following checklist to evaluate the competitors your business is likely to face. Be careful not to define your competitor too narrowly. For example, if you're considering opening a new movie theater, your competition isn't limited to other theaters. You'll also be competing with VCR rentals, bowling centers, and other forms of entertainment for the consumer's discretionary dollar.

- Who are your potential competitors?

- What are their strengths? Weaknesses?

- Who are the customers of each competitor?

- Why might a consumer buy from them instead of you?

- What is the approximate sales volume of each major competitor? Are there any significant trends in sales?

- What is the market share of each competitor?

- What is the cost structure of each competitor? Lower overhead? Higher?

- What is the pricing structure of each competitor? Below your products/services? Higher?

- Do competitors enjoy support from a strong franchise parent company?

- How do competitors promote their products, services?

- What are the distribution arrangements for major competitors?

- Who are the suppliers of each competitor?

- How is each competitor positioned? That is, what is the mental image that comes to the consumer's mind when s/he thinks of each competitor?

CONDUCT A SITUATION ANALYSIS
(Continued)

Analyze (Continued)

- Are there known potential future competitors not currently operating in the industry? If so, who?

- What are the management strengths/weaknesses of each major competitor?

- Are the competitors well financed?

- How committed is each competitor? That is, will competitors be forced to vigorously compete after you enter the market?

- Are future technological developments likely to alter your competitor's product line and/or mode of operation? Are they better prepared to adapt to change, or are you?

- How does each competitor's product line rate in terms of breadth and depth?

- How do competing products rate in terms of quality, size, appearance, durability, packaging, etc?

- What are the credit terms of major competitors with customers/suppliers?

- Do competitors "stand behind" their products? That is, how do their warranties rate?

- What sort of auxiliary services do competitors offer (e.g. gift wrapping, installation, delivery, maintenance and repair, etc.)? Are customers charged separately for these services?

- Do competitors own any patents or any exclusive distribution "rights" that would affect your market entry?

- If competitors are retail stores or service businesses, how do their physical facilities rate in terms of layout, decor, cleanliness, parking, convenience of location, ambiance, etc?

- What are their hours of operation?

- Within the community, how saturated is the competition? In other words, is there room for your new business?

STEP #2

Articulate Your Personal Objectives.

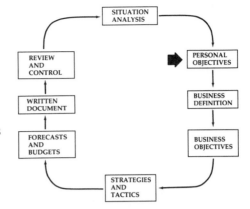

Owning and operating a business requires commitment and self-motivation. But commitment and self-motivation must be directed toward some objective, purpose, or rationale. If you have trouble articulating why you want to go into business, you may have trouble channeling your energies. Or you may find yourself going into business for the wrong reasons. Or you may have unrealistic expectations. The realities of long hours, hard work, and ultimate responsibilities of owning a business will quickly discourage the uncommitted entrepreneur who has not thoughtfully assessed what such a major decision entails.

To help you identify personal objectives, ask yourself the following questions:

- What is my primary motivation to start a business? Wealth, security, self-esteem, achievement, power, or social affiliation? Your personal objectives will influence your business objectives.

- How much risk am I willing to assume? Don't overlook the fact that risk can be social and psychological as well as monetary.

- How long and hard am I willing to work? Remember that your business isn't your only activity sphere. A personal policy will need to be developed to balance your role as an entrepreneur with your other roles (spouse, parent, citizen, church member, etc.).

- What is a reasonable timetable for my objectives? That is, what do you want your business to do for you in the first year of operation?...second, fifth, etc.?

- How will I know if I've reached my objectives? Ideally, your objectives should have deadlines, and be clearly stated, unambiguous, and quantified.

- Will I be able to ''survive'' if I fail to meet one or more of my objectives? If your business isn't as successful as you'd like, how will you know when it is time to get out of business?

- What kind of emotional support systems do I have? What kind do I need?

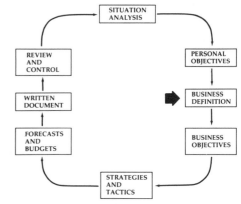

STEP #3

Define the Business.

This step in the planning process involves answering a seemingly obvious question: What business will I be in? By now you probably know what sort of business you're planning, but it is helpful to clearly delineate what you envision your business is or is not. Otherwise your business may take an identity of its own— with no clear direction of where it is going and no integrated effort for getting it there.

Ideally, try to define your business on the basis of the customers you plan to serve and type of goods and services you plan to offer. No business can survive if it fails to satisfy customer needs. Yet it is largely a business' goods and services that distinguish it from competitors and gives rise to consumer choice, so a product dimension is also relevant. When defining your business, consider these key questions:

1. **WHO** is the customer? Refer to the customer description you developed while conducting the situation analysis. If competitors are well entrenched, it may be wise to identify market niches the competition has ignored.

2. **WHAT** customer needs will be satisfied by the business? Needs may be broadly categorized as primary (viscerogenic—e.g. need for food, water, warmth, etc.) or secondary (psychogenic—e.g. need for status, achievement, social affiliation, knowledge, etc.). Properly engineered and positioned, most products are capable of satisfying several needs simultaneously.

3. **HOW** will the business satisfy customer needs? What goods? What services? What technologies? What processes?

When defining the business be careful not to be too narrow or too broad. Too narrow a focus may ignore potential opportunities (and competitors) while too broad a focus may fail to provide direction. Notice that possible answers to the "who," "what," and "how" questions posed above can range from very specific to very broad.

1. **WHO** is the customer?
   Examples: Individuals with a sweet tooth. Those who want to "munch". All consumers.

2. **WHAT** customer needs will be satisfied?
   Examples: Need for glucose. Need to quickly quench hunger in an enjoyable way. Need for self-treat.

3. **HOW** will the business satisfy customer needs?
   Examples: Manufacture sweet individually packaged snacks, provide good-tasting, between meal products. Provide consumers with food products.

> *Based upon the above examples, an appropriate business definition might be:*
> *We will manufacture and market good-tasting sweet snacks to enable individuals to quickly satisfy their hunger.*

STEP #4

Identify Your Business Objectives.

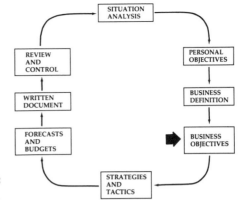

Businesses do not become successful by accident. Rather, the entrepreneur must establish objectives for the business. *Objectives* should be measurable and attainable benchmarks for goals. *Objectives* are usually expressed in terms of survival, growth, profitability, or revenues. For example, a business' *goal* may be "to maximize profitability," whereas the corresponding *objective* might be "to attain a 12% return on net worth during the initial year of operation." Such an objective is specific enough that an entrepreneur can continuously evaluate the business' progress and can take corrective action as necessary. To not have objectives or monitor progress is like bowling in the dark. You hear sounds of pins being struck (or missed), but there is no way of knowing the score. It would also be impossible to know what adjustments are required.

The definition and *goals* of a business may remain fairly stable over a long period of time. The business' *objectives* however are likely to vary reflecting changes in the environment and changes in the business' competitive posture.

On the next page, there are several examples of business objectives. It is probably wise to focus on only a few. Notice the characteristics of well-stated objectives. They tend to be:

- *Quantitative.* Most are expressed in precise numerical terms, although some objectives are inescapably qualitative.

- *Time-frame specific.* To specify a time frame for an objective is to hold yourself accountable.

- *Flexible.* If the business environment changes radically, you shouldn't be reluctant to adjust the level of your objectives or the time frame for their accomplishment.

- *Understandable.* If they're not clear to you (and your employees), you will have trouble reaching them.

- *Realistic.* Be honest with yourself (and with any potential investors). Otherwise you are asking for trouble.

- *Consistent.* Avoid multiple objectives that may be contradictory (e.g., "build market share" vs. "increase profitability per average order").

IDENTIFY YOUR BUSINESS OBJECTIVES
(Continued)

TYPES OF BUSINESS OBJECTIVES AND SELECTED EXAMPLES

Sales Objectives (e.g., total, by product, by customer segment, etc.)
    Dollar sales growth
    Unit sales growth
    Market Share
    Number of new accounts
    Average order size

> Examples: "Sell 1,000 units of product A and 500 units of product B by December 31, 19XX." "Maintain a minimum market share of 5% of all carbonated beverage sales in the Dallas/Fort Worth area during 19XX"

Financial Objectives*
    Return on Net Worth (RONW)
    Return on Sales (ROS)
    Return on Assets (ROA)
    Net Worth
    Inventory turnover
    Accounts receivable
    Working Capital

> Examples: "Attain an overall return on sales of at least 2% for 19XX." "Keep accounts receivable below 25% of net sales for any monthly period during the first three years of operation."

Other Objectives
    New equipment and processes
    New plants
    New offices
    Geographic expansion
    New product introductions
    Product quality
    Customer complaints
    Business image

> Examples: "Begin producing all of our own products by February 28, 19XX." "Beginning September 19XX resolve 95% of all complaints within two business days."

---

*See page 101 for some recommended books on business finance.

SET SPECIFIC OBJECTIVES

After reviewing the examples of business objectives on the previous page, it is understandable to ask questions such as ''How *high* a return on net worth should I shoot for?; What is an appropriate *level* of sales for my business?; How *many* times should my inventory turn over?; etc.'' Unfortunately there are no easy answers. The appropriate level of each objective depends on several factors, such as:

- Industry standards.
- Market potential.
- Access to capital.
- Type of business (e.g., manufacturing, retail, service, etc.).
- Strengths and weaknesses of the business.
- Nature and extensiveness of competition.
- The owner's aggressiveness and willingness to assume risk.
- The financial structure of the business (e.g., proportion of debt financing vs. equity financing).
- The cost structure of the business' products.
- Likely economic and industry trends.

There are, however, at least four general tools or approaches to utilize when setting business objectives. These include: 1) references to your personal objectives, 2) industry norms, 3) your break-even analysis, and 4) a strategic profit model. These are discussed on the next page.

4 THINGS TO CONSIDER

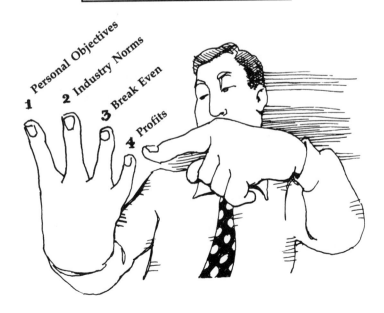

IDENTIFY YOUR BUSINESS OBJECTIVES (Continued)

Four Things to Consider When Setting Business Objectives

1. *Personal objectives.* These provide direction to help you decide how ambitious your business objectives should be, how much risk the business should assume, and what level of profitability the business should achieve.

2. *Industry norms.* Companies such as Dun and Bradstreet, Robert Morris and Associates, and specific industry trade associations publish financial ratios and other statistics for both specific companies and industries. Be careful when evaluating industry-wide data, however. These statistics aggregate the performances of poorly managed and struggling businesses with those of successful businesses.

3. *Break-even analysis.* Successful entrepreneurs are able to quickly assess the relationship between their costs, their revenues, and profitability. If you are able to estimate your costs and have some idea of the level of profitability you want to achieve, a break-even analysis can help you determine an appropriate sales goal. For example, suppose you estimate the following:

   $5,000.00 = monthly fixed or direct costs (e.g., rent, salaries, insurance, other overhead, etc.).
   $30.00 = average sale price of each unit.
   $10.00 = per unit variable cost of producing each unit.
   $2,500.00 = desired level of monthly profitability.

   Then, your monthly break-even point (or minimum number of monthly unit sales necessary to cover costs and desired profitability) would be computed as follows:

   $$\text{Break Even Point} = \frac{\$5000 + 2500}{\$30 - \$10} = 375 \text{ units per month}$$

4. *Strategic Profit Model.* A key long-term objective for most businesses involves return on net worth (RONW). This is defined as net profit after taxes, expressed as a percentage of the business' funds invested by the proprietor(s). As a primary measure of profitability, however, RONW is influenced by a number of intermediary determinants such as the rate of return on the total assets of the business and the degree of business leverage. These, in turn, are influenced by other considerations as shown on the facing page.

   The point is that there are many different ways to impact your RONW. Once you've set a target objective for your return, the strategic profit model can be useful in establishing a consistent set of objectives for the numerous components of RONW.

THE STRATEGIC PROFIT MODEL

Margin management	Asset management	Leverage management

Net profit margin

↓

$$\frac{\text{Net profits}}{\text{Net sales}}$$

Measures amount of net profit produced by each dollar of sales

×

Rate of asset turnover

↓

$$\frac{\text{Net sales}}{\text{Total assets}}$$

Measures dollars of sales volume produced by each dollar invested in total assets of business

Rate of return on assets (ROA)

↓

$$\frac{\text{Net profits}}{\text{Total assets}}$$

Measure for managers of return on all funds invested in business (by both owners and creditors)

×

Leverage ratio

↓

$$\frac{\text{Total assets}}{\text{Net worth}}$$

Dollars of total assets that can be acquired or supported for each dollar of owners' investment

Rate of return on net worth (RONW)

↓

$$\frac{\text{Net profits}}{\text{Net worth}}$$

Measure of profitability for owners who have provided net worth funds

Source: *Modern Retailing: Theory and Practice 4th ed*, by J. Barry Mason and Morris L. Mayer, Plano, TX: Business Publications, Inc. 1987, page 347.

Starting Your New Business: A Guide For Entrepreneurs

STEP #5

Formulate Business Strategies and Tactics.

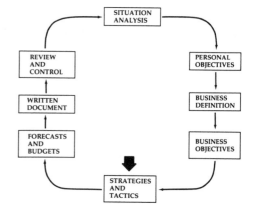

> "Strategy is the company's concept of how to win the war. Tactics are derived activities designed to win battles."
>
> Philip Kotler

The identification of business objectives (Step #4) establishes benchmarks for the business' performance. The next step is to develop specific action plans which will enable the business to reach those objectives. Broadly speaking, this will entail both strategies and tactics. Whereas this chapter will generally examine strategies and tactics simultaneously, Kotler's quote above implies a distinction between the two:

- *STRATEGIES* are the *major* courses of action a business utilizes to pursue its objectives.

- *TACTICS* are the *secondary* courses of action that will help support or implement the strategies.

So, for example, if sales growth is the key objective of the business, then the growth strategy might involve adding additional products to the product line. An appropriate tactic in this example might include hiring a consultant to systematically solicit and screen ideas for new products.

The initial objective a budding entrepreneur usually faces is simply to get the business open and begin operations. Consequently, most of the early organizational and operational decisions are actually strategic and tactical choices. These choices involve at least seven different areas:

1. **ORGANIZATION**
2. **PERSONNEL**
3. **PRODUCTION**
4. **PURCHASING**
5. **RECORD KEEPING**
6. **MARKETING**
7. **RISK MANAGEMENT (INSURANCE)**

Each decision area will be examined in greater depth in the next few pages.

STRATEGIC CONSIDERATION 1
ORGANIZATION

1. **Legal Structure.** A decision must be made as to the legal structure of the business. That is, will it be a sole proprietorship, a partnership, or a corporation? Antonio M. Olmi of the Small Business Administration recommends that budding entrepreneurs answer the following eight questions when choosing a legal structure:

   1. What is the size of the risk? That is, what is the amount of the investors' liability for debts and taxes?

   2. What would the continuity (life) of the firm be if something happened to the principal or principals?

   3. What legal structure would insure the greatest adaptability of administration for the firm?

   4. What are the influence of applicable laws?

   5. What are the possibilities of attracting additional capital?

   6. What are the needs for and possibilities of attracting additional expertise?

   7. What are the costs and procedures in starting?

   8. What is the ultimate goal and purpose of the enterprise, and which legal structure can best serve its purpose?

   The advantages and disadvantages of each form of legal structure (i.e., sole proprietorship, partnership or corporation) are outlined on the next two pages.

ORGANIZATION (Continued) ⬛ 1

Sole Proprietorships | A business owned by only one person.

Advantages
- Ease of formation.
- Sole ownership of profits.
- Control and decision making vested in one owner.
- Flexibility.
- Relative freedom from government control and special taxation.

Disadvantages
- Unlimited liability.
- Unstable business life (e.g. if owner should die).
- Less available capital, ordinarily, than in other types of business structures.
- Relative difficulty in obtaining long-term financing.
- Relatively limited viewpoint and experience of proprietor.

Partnerships | A business owned by two or more persons.

Advantages
- Ease of formation.
- Direct rewards.
- Growth and performance facilitated.
- Flexibility.
- Relative freedom from government control and special taxation.

Disadvantages
- Unlimited liability of at least one partner.
- Unstable life of business (e.g. if one owner should die).
- Relative difficulty in obtaining large sums of capital.
- Firm bound by the acts of just one partner as agent.
- Difficulty of disposing of partnership interest (e.g., if one partner wanted to buy out the other partner).

| Corporations | (A legal entity distinct from those parties or individuals that own it.)

Advantages
- The stockholder's liability is limited to a fixed investment amount.
- Ownership is readily transferable.
- Separate legal existence.
- Stability and relative permanence of existence.
- Relative ease of securing capital from many investor sources.
- The ability of the corporation to draw on the expertise and skills of more than one individual.

Disadvantages
- Activities limited by the charter and by various laws.
- Possible manipulation of minority stockholders.
- Extensive government regulations and required local, state, and federal reports.
- Less incentive if manager does not share in profits.
- Expense of forming a corporation.
- Double taxation (i.e., income tax on corporate net income and on individual salary and dividends).

NOTE: Double taxation can be avoided by selecting a "Subchapter S status." And in at least six states (Wyoming, Colorado, Florida, Kansas, Virginia, and Utah) there's another option that avoids double taxation and offers other attractive advantages as well. It is a *Limited Liability Company* or LLC for short.

| Franchises |

Another increasingly popular alternative for prospective small business owners is the franchise. Today there are more than 550,000 franchise outlets in the U.S. Many well known businesses are at least partially franchise operations: McDonald's and Hardee's (fast foods), Jazzercise (fitness clubs), Fantastic Sam's (hair care), and Maaco (auto painting).

Typically franchisors have fine-tuned the business operation before attempting to sell franchise units, and they usually provide helpful assistance to franchisees to keep the number of mistakes and mishaps to a minimum. Because of this assistance, becoming a franchisee is an attractive alternative for budding entrepreneurs who have never before owned a business. However, if you're very independent or very creative, you may not be happy as a franchisee—following the franchisor's policies and procedures. And, like any new business venture, franchise opportunities should be carefully evaluated. Incorporate the following questions in your investigation.

ORGANIZATION (Continued) 1

EVALUATING FRANCHISE OPPORTUNITIES

Who is the franchisor?

- How long has the franchisor been in the industry?

- How long has the firm granted franchises?

- How many franchises are there? How many in your area?

- What's the franchisor's attitude toward you? Is the firm concerned about your qualifications? Has the franchisor tried to rush you to sign the agreement?

- Are franchisees required to purchase supplies from the franchisor? If so, are prices competitive with other suppliers?

- What, if any, restrictions apply to competition with other franchisees?

- What are the terms covering renewal rights, and reselling the franchise?

- What is the reputation and image of the franchisor and his products?

Investigate the above questions by:

- Visiting the franchisor's headquarters.

- Asking the franchisor for a copy of the F.T.C.-required disclosure document.

- Talking to...
  —Current franchisees
  —Small Business Administration
  —Federal Trade Commission
  —Better Business Bureau
  —Chamber of Commerce
  —International Franchise Association
    (1025 Connecticut Ave., N.W., Washington, D.C. 20036).
  —Your lawyer.
  —Your accountant.

Source: *Evaluating Franchise Opportunities,* U.S. Small Business Administration, Management Aid #7.007, 1985.

ORGANIZATION STRUCTURE

Another organizational concern is how responsibility and work assignments will be handled in your business. If you have no partners, no employees, and no consultants, the answer is simple; you will do everything yourself. But, if your business will be more than a one person operation, then you'll have to select an organizational structure to make sure the business runs efficiently. The form of organizational structure you select will affect the way your staff works together, and how efficiently and effectively tasks are performed. A useful exercise is to design an organizational chart such as those shown below:

Line Organization

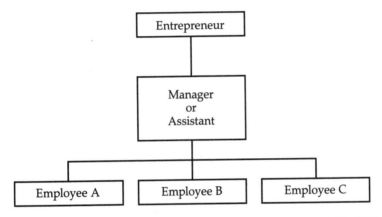

Appropriate when: Jobs are simple and routine; few employees; entrepreneur can stay in complete control.

Functional Organization

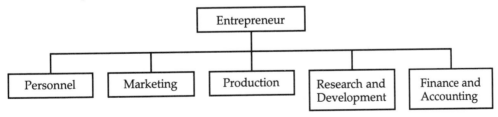

Appropriate when: Need for efficiency is important; several employees; the business environment is fairly stable.

ORGANIZATION (Continued) 1

Geographic Organization

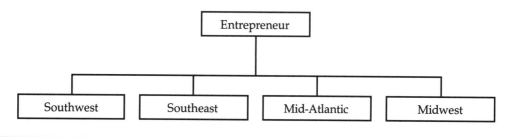

Appropriate when: Business operations are geographically dispersed; customer preferences and/or competition varies from one area to the next.

Product Specialization

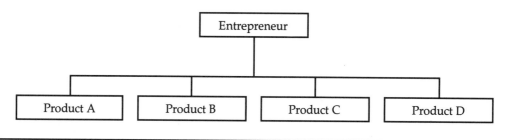

Appropriate when: Business offers several different unrelated products.

Customer Organization

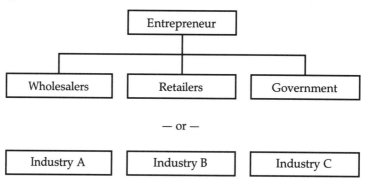

Appropriate when: Needs and appeals vary from one customer group to the next.

In their zeal to launch their business, entrepreneurs may plan start-up organizations, but few develop contingency plans for later reorganizations and ''what ifs.'' For example, consider the following questions that might be relevant to your new business.

- In a partnership, what will happen to the business if one of the partners suddenly becomes ill, disabled, dies, retires, or simply loses interest in the business and wants out? Who will assume the partner's duties in the business and how will that person be compensated? Will the leaving partner or his heirs have any rights to assets, copyrights, patents, or future profits, and how will the value of these be determined? Are partners obligated to buy one another's share of the business, and if so, under what circumstances? How will the proceeds of the business be divided if the business is sold?

- Similarly, in a sole proprietorship, what happens to the business if you suddenly die? As founder, does your will address who should run the business and how business assets or earnings should be distributed to beneficiaries? If you divorce, what claims will your spouse have on assets and future earnings of the business?

- If you plan to pass the business on to another family member, or to someone else, when and how will the transition be handled? How will the sale price be determined? Will you have any role in the business after ownership is passed?

Of course it is impossible to fully anticipate and plan for every possible twist of fate the future might hold, but some forethought can help to avoid bitter disagreements between partners, burdensome courtroom battles, excessive taxes, family disputes and other hardships. With the help of an attorney and an accountant, draw up a buy-sell agreement, establish a trust or estate freeze, revise your will, or try some combination of these suggestions. At the very least, talk with partners and other relevant parties, try to reach a concensus and commit the agreement to paper. Then periodically review the document to keep it current.

STRATEGIC CONSIDERATION PERSONNEL 2

STAFFING

Most strategic and tactical staffing decisions for small businesses tend to revolve around the following five questions:

1. What type of employees are needed?

2. How many employees are needed?

3. How should potential employees be recruited and screened?

4. How should employees be trained?

5. How should employees be compensated and motivated?

Evaluation of each employee's job performance is another important consideration, though not of immediate concern in opening the business.

To determine the type and number of employees needed, conduct a job analysis. That is, think through the requirements of each employee's job. Some job tasks may be grouped together so that employees performing those tasks need not be as highly skilled (or as highly paid) as employees who will perform other tasks. Organizing jobs in this fashion could reduce the business' payroll costs and increase work efficiency. On the other hand it could limit employee scheduling flexibility. Customer service might also suffer. Upon completion of each job analysis, write job descriptions and job specifications for each job as described below:

— **Job Description:** Formal, written statement describing the nature of the specific job, its requirements, and its responsibilities (see example, on page 41).

— **Job Specification:** Statement converting job description into people qualifications. That is, what abilities, skills, level of education, and experience are necessary for an employee to perform successfully in the specific job (see example, on page 42).

SAMPLE JOB DESCRIPTION

POSITION TITLE: Snack Bar Attendant

Purpose: To sell, prepare and serve food and beverages to customers.

Duties:
1. Prepare food according to established methods and portions.

2. Operate cash register and complete food checks, where applicable.

3. Maintain immaculate cleanliness of all snack bar areas and ensure hygienic conditions.

4. Maintain refrigerator, freezer and inventories in an orderly and clean manner.

5. Clear and clean tables.

6. Set tables, where applicable.

7. Clean and fill napkin and condiment containers.

8. Requisition and receive food and supplies, where applicable.

9. Arrange display of food on back counter, where applicable.

10. Adhere to Board of Health regulations.

11. Insure Alcoholic Beverage Commission regulations are honored.

12. Clean entire snack bar area at end of shift.

13. Other duties as assigned.

Directs Work Of: (Not applicable)

Responsibility: This position is responsible for specific routine assignments under direct supervision.

Source: *Bowling Center Job Descriptions,* Arlington, TX: The Bowling Proprietors Association of America.

PERSONNEL (Continued) 2

SAMPLE JOB SPECIFICATION

POSITION TITLE: Snack Bar Attendant

Education: Eighth Grade.

Experience: Experience of six months in food and beverage service preferred. If required to handle alcoholic beverages, see local regulations regarding age.

Knowledge: Able to operate a cash register. Basic knowledge of food and beverage preparation procedures.

Judgment: Minimal use of judgment is required because the duties to be performed are based on established procedures and direct instruction. Problems are referred to a higher level for solution.

Source: *Bowling Center Job Descriptions,* Arlington, TX: The Bowling Proprietors Association of America.

SCREENING APPLICANTS

Classified advertisements, employment agencies, college placement offices, trade associations, trade journals, and word-of-mouth advertising are a few potential sources for generating job applicants. Of course, not every applicant will be qualified, so a combination of the following tools to screen applicants should be used.

1. *Application blanks* provide an inexpensive way to screen applicants who are clearly not qualified. Application blanks can be structured to emphasize the key job qualifications determined in the job analysis.

2. *Resumés* are an alternative to application blanks. Because organization will vary from applicant to applicant, it may be difficult to objectively compare and contrast potential employees.

3. *Employment references* usually provide some indication of applicants' "intangible" qualities—e.g. responsibility, punctuality, demeanor, work attitudes, and ability to work with others. These days many employers will hesitate to speak negatively about former employees. The question "Would you hire this person again?" will often screen undesirable applicants.

4. *Interviews* are useful in assessing applicants' interpersonal and communication skills. These are especially important if the job involves working with others. It is sometimes difficult to objectively evaluate other skills. The interview questions on the facing page should help you select the best candidates.

PERSONNEL (Continued) 2

SCREENING APPLICANTS (Continued)

USEFUL JOB INTERVIEW QUESTIONS

1. What are your long range and short range goals? Why did you establish these goals and how are you preparing yourself to achieve them?

2. What specific goals, other than those related to your occupation, have you established for yourself for the next five years?

3. What do you *really* want to do in life?

4. Why are you interested in this job?

5. Which is more important money or a job you genuinely enjoy?

6. What do you consider to be your greatest strengths and weaknesses?

7. How would a friend describe you?

8. What motivates you to put forth your greatest effort?

9. How has your education prepared you to work in a job like the one that is available?

10. Why should I hire you?

11. In what ways do you think you can make a contribution to this business?

12. Do you have plans to continue your education?

13. How do you work under pressure?

14. Which previous jobs have been most interesting? Why?

15. What things are most important to you in a job?

16. Are you willing to spend time as a trainee?

Source: Adapted from materials supplied by the College Placement Office, West Texas State University, Canyon, TX.

5. *Employment tests* can be used to assess each applicant's aptitude, personality, knowledge, and interests. Professionally developed tests are recommended because their validity has been established. Detailed information regarding employment tests may be obtained from local college guidance and testing centers.

6. *Honesty tests* are helpful in screening applicants. There are some paper and pencil assessments available that tend to be more convenient, less expensive, and legally less restrictive than polygraph devices.

Training

Once selected, each employee must be trained. This may involve on-the-job training or any of the following:

—Lectures, seminars, college or adult education courses, written procedures manuals, on-site demonstrations, videotapes/audiotapes, and self-study books like this one

Compensation

The ability to pay competitive wages will affect the quality of your employees. Keep in mind, however, that the total cost of compensation can exceed direct wages by 40% or more when you include:

—employer's contribution to social security
—unemployment compensation, workman's compensation and
   disability insurance
—sick leave, vacations, holidays
—major medical and/or life insurance
—pension contributions and/or retirement plans
—profit-sharing plans, bonus agreements or deferred compensation

When designing a compensation program, consider the motivational potential of the *method* of pay vs. the *level* of pay. A sales person may be more motivated when paid a $4.00 commission per unit with a monthly sales quota of 500 units, than when paid a straight monthly salary of $2000. Other financial incentives can also be motivational (e.g. sales contests, special awards, bonuses, etc.).

STRATEGIC CONSIDERATION 3
PRODUCTION

PRODUCTION DECISIONS

Production decisions involve the processes by which tangible goods are manufactured and intangible services are provided. These decisions play a key role in the overall business strategy because product quality, cash flow, control, costs, and continuity of supply are all affected by the production alternatives selected.

Several production decisions should be contemplated prior to the business start-up. For example:

1. *Will tangible goods be manufactured or purchased?* It is tempting to believe that manufacturing products will save you money. This is not always the case. Consider the technical expertise, quality and dependability other manufacturers have. Also consider the initial fixed costs that are required.

   A practical alternative might be to first purchase from other manufacturers; and later (perhaps) produce the items yourself. Or, consider purchasing major component parts from others and doing the final assembly. If you're not certain whether to "make or buy," examine the points below before you decide to do the manufacturing.

2. *What is your desired level of capacity?* How many items would you like to produce? This decision will impact the amount of physical space needed, the number of employees and quality of equipment required. High-capacity operations often enjoy economies of scale but have higher initial costs. Conversely, low-capacity operations tend to have higher variable costs, but lower fixed costs and greater flexibility of production.

3. *What raw materials, equipment and supplies will be needed in the manufacturing process?* Are they readily available at a reasonable price? Can equipment be leased or purchased? (Note: See page 47 for additional information.)

Example of a Production Operations Flow Chart For the Manufacture of Pencil Holders

PRODUCTION (Continued) 3

PRODUCTION DECISIONS (Continued)

4. *What operations are required in the production process?* What is the sequence of those operations and how much time will be needed for each? Could operations be combined, eliminated, accelerated, or sub-contracted? These considerations will impact the layout, the space needed, the number of employees, the skills needed, and the scheduling of production runs.

   A useful exercise is to develop a production operations flow chart such as the one on the facing page.

   Keep in mind that production operations, equipment, and facilities must comply with the Occupational Safety and Health Act (OSHA) of 1970. Write the U.S. Government Printing Office for a copy of *Standards for General Industry.*

5. *How much space will be needed?* In addition to the plant facilities alluded to above, also plan necessary space for the storage of raw materials, supplies, tools, component parts and finished goods. Additional space for restrooms, employee lunch areas, employee/visitor parking, an office, and possible future expansion should also be considered.

6. *What level of quality is desired?* How will quality be measured? How will consistent quality be maintained? Who will be responsible for delivering quality? Entrepreneurs often assume that high quality standards are expensive and that customers will be unwilling to pay for quality. While these concerns are sometimes justified, it is often more expensive in the long-run to sacrifice quality. Inadequate quality creates dissatisfied customers who may take their patronage elsewhere and be costly to replace. Or, unhappy customers may return defective merchandise for expensive repair or replacement, tell their friends and family not to buy your ''shoddy products,'' or complain to the retailer who may stop ordering from you in the future.

BONUS OFFER: For a *free* guide to implementing a quality improvement program in your new business, contact the National Institute of Standards and Technology (Route 270 and Quince Orchard Road, Administration Building, Room A537, Gaithersburg, Maryland 20899, Phone: 301-975-2036). Ask for a copy of the application guidelines for the Malcolm Baldrige National Quality Award.

STRATEGIC CONSIDERATION PURCHASING AND INVENTORY CONTROL 4

PURCHASING CONSIDERATIONS

Effective and efficient purchasing and inventory systems are mandatory. Savings from these functions often go directly to the bottom line. That is, a $1000 decrease in purchasing or inventory costs will increase net profit by $1000. It would take a five-fold (or more) increase in sales to generate a similar increase in profit. Moreover, a well managed purchasing and inventory system can minimize the headaches and lost revenues associated with substandard resale items, raw materials, and supplies, as well as problems of late deliveries, stock-outs, and obsolete merchandise. Barker, Hovey and Murphy* offer the following seven key questions to consider when establishing a purchasing system:

1. Have you established specific policies regarding who is authorized to purchase goods or services? Place requisitions? Process records?

2. Have you discussed your purchasing requirements with other firms or local trade associations to obtain suggestions and/or techniques?

3. Have you requested prices from several vendors for each item or service you will purchase?

4. Have you visited or investigated potential vendors to verify that they can meet your requirements in terms of price, quality, quantity and service?

5. Does the volume of purchasing for any item warrant your dealing directly with the manufacturer, rather than with middlemen?

6. Do your vendors have regular and competent sales personnel?

7. Do you anticipate problems with suppliers with regard to shortages? Backdoor selling? Delivery delays? Unsolicited favors or gifts?

---

*Source: *Management Audit for Small Service Firms,* Phillis A. Barker, David H. Hovey, and John J. Murphy, Washington, D.C.: U.S. Small Business Administration, 1976, pp. 37-39.

INVENTORY CONSIDERATIONS

When planning inventory levels, consider the "hidden" costs in keeping too much inventory on hand. These include:

1. *Financing costs*—the interest expense associated with purchases.
2. *Opportunity costs*—alternative income-producing use of the money tied-up in inventory.
3. *Insurance costs*—which increase as more inventory is carried.
4. *Storage costs*—when the space to store inventory must be leased or purchased.
5. *Obsolescence costs*—the lost sales that occur when "new and improved" models are introduced and consumers no longer want the "old" items in your inventory.
6. *Shrinkage costs*—losses due to breakage, damage, spoilage, or theft. The longer an item sits in inventory, the greater the likelihood of shrinkage.

Although excessive inventories can be costly, so can insufficient inventories. Shortages may mean frequent reordering (and higher attendant costs) or lost sales (and dissatisfied customers). To balance the tradeoff between insufficient and excessive inventories, a powerful tool has been developed which is called the economic order quantity or EOQ. The EOQ is the most economical number of units to be purchased per order. The ideal inventory level for each item should never dramatically exceed the EOQ. An EOQ is computed as follows:

$$EOQ = \sqrt{\frac{2SV}{IC}}$$ which simply means:

S = the estimated annual sales (in units)
V = the variable costs to place an order
I = Inventory holding costs, as a percentage of average inventory
C = Cost of one item

Therefore, if S = 1000 units, V = $20, I = .20 holding cost, and C = $30 for the cost of one item.

Then:

$$EOQ = \sqrt{\frac{(2)(1000)(20)}{(.2)(30)}} = 81.66$$

The ideal would be therefore to order about 82 units each time the inventory is replenished.

STRATEGIC CONSIDERATION 5
RECORD KEEPING

SELECTING PAPERWORK
AND ACCOUNTING PROCEDURES

Although some record keeping decisions could be postponed until after the start-up, determining in advance what paperwork and accounting records are needed will save time and headaches in the long-run. Record keeping is important in a strategic and tactical context because it will affect:

—the way employees perform their jobs
—the accountability of employees
—the quality of customer service
—an owner's ability to monitor business operations
—the quality of the decision making
—the ability to raise additional capital
—long-term planning, and ultimately . . .
—profitability and success.

Specific Record Keeping Needs

These will vary from business to business, but every system should provide needed and meaningful information. Systems should also be easy to use and understand, reliable, inexpensive, accurate, consistent, and timely. A record keeping system might typically include records for the following:

Business Records to Maintain

1. Sales
2. Cash receipts/Cash disbursements
3. Accounts receivable/accounts payable
4. Physical assets (including depreciation)
5. Insurance
6. Personnel (including payroll)
7. Customers and potential customers
8. Suppliers and other creditors
9. Production and inventory
10. Miscellaneous correspondence

The facing page provides a financial status check list to assist a small businessperson to assess whether or not the financial bookkeeping system used is providing adequate information. There are numerous commercial systems (hard copy and software) available to help you keep track of your financial records. Your accountant and/or local office supply store will give you recommendations.

Some non-financial records also have great value—i.e. employee performance evaluations, customer inquiries and complaints, insurance policies, supplier information and so on.

SMALL BUSINESS FINANCIAL RECORDS CHECKLIST

(WHAT AN OWNER—MANAGER SHOULD KNOW)

DAILY

- ☐ Cash on hand.
- ☐ Bank Balance (keep business and personal funds separate).
- ☐ Daily Summary of sales and cash receipts.
- ☐ All errors in recording collections on accounts are corrected.
- ☐ That a record of all monies paid out, by cash or check, is maintained.

WEEKLY

- ☐ Accounts Receivable (take action on slow payers).
- ☐ Accounts Payable (take advantage of discounts).
- ☐ Payroll (records should include name and address of employee, social security number, number of exemptions, date ending the pay period, hours worked, rate of pay, total wages, deductions, net pay, check number).
- ☐ Taxes and reports to State and Federal Government (sales, withholding, social security, etc.)

MONTHLY

- ☐ All Journal entries are classified according to like elements (these should be generally accepted and standardized for both income and expense) and posted to General Ledger.
- ☐ That a Profit and Loss Statement for the month is available within a reasonable time, (10 to 15 days following the close of the month). This shows the income for the business for the month, the expense incurred in obtaining the income, and the resulting profit or loss.

(Continued on next page)

SMALL BUSINESS FINANCIAL RECORDS CHECKLIST (Continued)

(WHAT AN OWNER—MANAGER SHOULD KNOW)

MONTHLY (Continued)

☐ That a Balance Sheet accompanies the Profit and Loss Statement. This shows assets (what the business has), liabilities (what the business owes), and the investment of the owner.

☐ That the Bank Statement is reconciled. (That is, the owner's books are in agreement with the bank's record of the cash balance.)

☐ That Petty Cash is in balance, (the actual cash in the Petty Cash Box plus the total of the paid-out slips that have not been charged to expense total the amount set aside as petty cash).

☐ That all Federal Tax Deposits, Withheld income and FICA Taxes (form 501) and State Taxes have been made.

☐ That age of Accounts Receivables are known, i.e., 30, 60, 90 days, etc., past due. (Work to resolve all bad and slow paying accounts.)

☐ That Inventory Control is worked to remove dead stock and order new stock. (What moves slowly? Reduce. What moves fast? Increase.)

YOU CAN DO IT!

FINANCIAL RECORDS

Source: *Keeping Records in Small Business*, John Cotton, U.S. Small Business Administration, Management Aid #1.017, 1985

STRATEGIC CONSIDERATION MARKETING 6

MARKETING ACTIVITIES

Marketing involves the exchange of valued goods and services for money. Properly done, both the customer and the business will benefit. Marketing activities are those that facilitate the exchange process. Most marketing decisions the small business person faces may be grouped into five broad categories, with marketing research (previously discussed) being the tool to ensure the quality of these decisions. These categories include:

1. Selection of target markets
2. Product
3. Pricing
4. Promotion
5. Distribution

TARGET MARKETS

It is usually a mistake to try to be all things to all people. Most successful businesses select one (or a few) potential customer groups (i.e. *target markets*) and focus marketing efforts on these groups. A separate marketing program may be necessary for each group. Select target markets on the basis of your ability to serve them relative to that of your competition. Of course, target markets should be substantial enough to be profitable.

PRODUCT

A *product* is more than simply a tangible object. For many service businesses there is little or nothing tangible about the product that is offered. Rather, a product is a *bundle of benefits* offered to the customer. This bundle might include the object's physical properties such as style, distinctive features, options, colors, and quality, but equally important are benefits such as delivery, installation, warranty, usage instructions, and so on. Decisions concerning the composition of the benefit bundle are marketing-relevant because they are directly tied to the customer's satisfaction with the business. Shoddy or inappropriate products turn off customers and, in the long run, cannot be offset by reduced prices, increased advertising, or substitute efforts.

MARKETING (Continued)   6

PRICING

Pricing decisions extend far beyond determining that the product should sell for $30, $40, or some other amount. For example, what about discounts for early payments, promotional assistance, or quantity purchases? How long will each credit customer have to pay (*if* some customers are granted credit)? Will the business accept checks, major credit cards or bartering?

When formulating a comprehensive pricing philosophy, also consider the following:

—*Cost.* In the long term your prices must more than cover your costs of doing business.

—*Competition.* What does the competition offer and how much do they charge?

—*Systems price.* What is the total price the customer must pay to acquire your product, including postage/freight, personal transportation, parking, long distance phone charges, baby-sitting, etc.? Might there be ways to minimize these expenses to make your product more competitive?

—*Market demand.* How price sensitive are potential customers? What are their perceptions of a fair price?

—*Communication.* How well will the other elements of the marketing arsenal be used to communicate pricing decisions (e.g., increases as well as decreases) to customers?

—*Non-monetary price.* How much time, inconvenience, or anxiety must customers pay to acquire and use your products?

—*Objectives.* For example, lower prices might be necessary to gain a strong foothold in the marketplace and to deter would-be competitors. Conversely, higher prices might be appropriate if you're trying to foster an air of product exclusivity and prestige.

PROMOTION

Contrary to popular belief, if you build a better mousetrap, the world will *not* necessarily beat a path to your door. Regardless of the superiority of your product(s), a consumer is not motivated to purchase until s/he is at least informed of its availability. And it is with the use of promotional tools that the entrepreneur must assume the responsibility to inform consumers.

Dozens of promotional alternatives exist. Each has distinctive advantages and disadvantages. Broadly categorized, promotional tools include:

—*Advertising* (i.e., paid and non-personal communication usually directed toward a mass audience by an identified business). Radio, television, magazines, direct mail, and billboards are common advertising media.

—*Personal selling* (i.e. oral presentation to prospective customers with intent of making a sale). Personal selling is especially useful for closing the sale after advertising has heightened a customer's awareness.

—*Sales promotion* (i.e., short-term inducements to stimulate traffic and/or sales). Coupons, sweepstakes, point-of-purchase displays, rub-off cards, and free gifts are examples of commonly used sales promotions.

—*Publicity* (i.e., stimulation of awareness and interest through mass media and through individuals who are usually not directly paid by the business). News items, announcements, and stories about the business, its new products, and its employees generate publicity — as do word-of-mouth communications that spread from customer to customer. Solid relations with the community, media, and customers generally enhance favorable publicity.

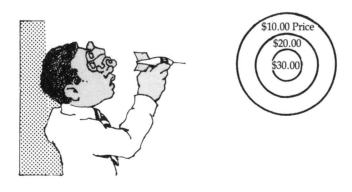

"HOW NOT TO SET A PRICE"

MARKETING (Continued) 6

DISTRIBUTION

Distribution decisions involve those activities that move the product from the seller to the ultimate consumer. These include:

—*Location* of business, especially for most retail and service firms (see location and site selection previously discussed under "situation analysis" page 21).

—*Channel selection.* A company that is able to coordinate a network of wholesalers, retailers and other middlemen can often gain market access quicker, more efficiently, more extensively, and with less expense and less risk than might otherwise be possible. Multiple channels, however, may be difficult to control. The chart on the facing page illustrates some common channels of distribution.

—*Intensity.* Distribution might be intensive if your objective is to make the product widely available to gain market share, or if consumers are typically not brand loyal to products in the product category. On the other hand, a more selective or even exclusive distribution strategy is more appropriate if your product will be truly unique, have a prestige image, be highly sought by customers, and/or your manufacturing capacity is limited.

—*Physical transport.* You will need to answer questions such as: How will the product be shipped to middlemen and customers (e.g., freight, rail, air, etc.)? How quickly does the product need to be shipped (e.g., overnight express, next week, etc.)? What are the economical minimum quantity shipments? How must the products be packaged for shipment? Etc...

Page 60 describes a "perfect" working relationship between a manufacturer and a middleman.

EXAMPLES OF COMMON DISTRIBUTION CHANNELS

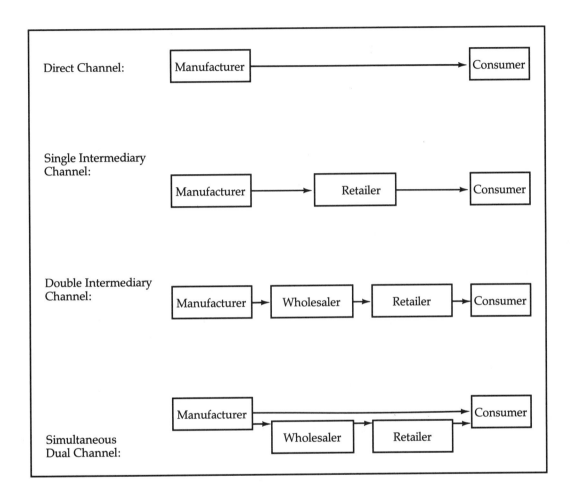

MARKETING (Continued) 6

MANUFACTURERS AND MIDDLEMEN: A PERFECT WORKING RELATIONSHIP

The perfect middleman:

1. Has access to the market that the manufacturer wants to reach.

2. Carries an adequate inventory of the manufacturer's products and a satisfactory assortment of other products.

3. Has an effective promotional program—advertising, personal selling, and product displays. Promotional demands placed on the manufacturer are in line with what the manufacturer intends to do.

4. Provides services to customers—credit, delivery, installation, and product repair—and honors the product warranty conditions.

The perfect manufacturer:

1. Provides a desirable assortment of products—well designed, properly priced, attractively packaged, and delivered on time and in adequate quantities.

2. Builds product demand for these products by advertising their unique features and benefits.

3. Furnishes promotional assistance to its middlemen.

4. Provides managerial assistance for its middlemen.

5. Honors product warranties and provides repair and installation service.

The perfect combination:

1. Probably doesn't exist.

Source: Adapted from *Fundamentals of Marketing*, 8th ed., William J. Stanton and Charles Futrell, New York: McGraw Hill, 1987, p. 380.

STRATEGIC CONSIDERATION 7
MANAGING RISK

INSURANCE

"Where profit is, loss is hidden nearby."—Japanese Proverb

Risk is an accepted reality in American business. It is omni-present. Some entrepreneurs thrive upon risk, finding it to provide excitement and challenge. Others find it to be anxiety-producing and the potential for loss associated with risk to be intolerable.

Risk can often be reduced. For example, learning a customer's needs will reduce the risk of offering a product no one will purchase. Adopting safety measures will reduce the risk of fire or injury. In instances where the risk can't be totally avoided, it usually can be transferred to someone else—through insurance, for example. Before opening a business you should consult with a few insurance agents about your business insurance needs. Otherwise you may be risking more than you can afford to lose.

According to the Small Business Administration, four types of insurance are essential, while nine other types may be desirable—depending on the business and the entrepreneur's aversion to risk.

ESSENTIAL INSURANCE

1. **FIRE**
2. **LIABILITY**
3. **AUTOMOBILE**
4. **WORKER'S COMPENSATION**

DESIRABLE INSURANCE

— Business Interruption
— Crime
— Glass
— Rent
— Group Life
— Group Health
— Disability
— Retirement Income
— Key-Man

The next several pages provide key considerations associated with each kind of insurance coverage.

ESSENTIAL INSURANCE COVERAGE CHECKLIST

	No action needed	*Look into this*

FIRE INSURANCE

1. Other perils—such as windstorm, hail, smoke, explosion, vandalism, and malicious mischief—can be added to your basic fire insurance at a relatively small additional cost.

2. If you need comprehensive coverage, your best buy may be one of the all-risk contracts that offer the broadest available protection for the money.

3. The insurance company may indemnify you—that is, compensate you for your losses—in any one of several ways: (1) It may pay actual cash value of the property at the time of loss, (2) it may repair or replace the property with material of like kind and quality, or (3) it may take all the property at the agreed or appraised value and reimburse you for your loss.

4. You can insure property you do not own. You must have an insurable interest—that is, a financial interest—in the property when a loss occurs but not necessarily at the time the insurance contract is made. For instance, a repair shop or a dry-cleaning plant may carry insurance on customers' property in the shop, or a person holding a mortgage on a building may insure the building although he or she does not own it.

5. When you sell property, you cannot assign the insurance policy along with the property unless you have permission from the insurance company.

6. Even if you have several policies on your property, you can still collect only the amount of your actual cash loss. All the insurers share the payment proportionately. For example, suppose that you are carrying two policies—one for $20,000 and one for $30,000—on a $40,000 building, and a fire causes damage to the building amounting to $12,000.

   The $20,000 policy will pay $4,800; that is:

   $$\frac{20,000}{50,000} \text{ or } \frac{2}{5}, \text{ of } \$12,000 = \$4,800$$

   The $30,000 policy will pay $7,200; which is:

   $$\frac{30,000}{50,000} \text{ or } \frac{3}{5}, \text{ of } \$12,000 = \$7,200$$

7. Special protection other than the standard fire policy is needed to cover the loss by fire of accounts, bills, currency, deeds, evidences of debt, and money and securities.

FIRE INSURANCE *(Continued)*

8. If an insured building is vacant or unoccupied for more than sixty consecutive days, coverage is suspended unless you have a special endorsement to your policy canceling this provision.

9. If, either before or after a loss, you conceal or misrepresent to the insurer any material fact or circumstance concerning your insurance or the interest of the insured, the policy may be voided.

10. If you increase the hazard of fire, the insurance company may suspend your coverage even for losses not originating from the increased hazard. (An example of such a hazard might be renting part of your building to a dry-cleaning plant.)

11. After a loss, you must use all reasonable means to protect the property from further loss, or run the risk of having your coverage canceled.

12. To recover your loss, you must furnish—within sixty days (unless an extension is granted by the insurance company)—a complete inventory of the damaged, destroyed, and undamaged property showing in detail quantities, costs, actual cash value, and amount of loss claimed.

13. If you and the insurer disagree on the amount of loss, the question may be resolved through special appraisal procedures provided for in the insurance policy.

14. You may cancel your policy without notice at any time and get part of the premium returned. The insurance company also may cancel at any time but it must give you a five-day written notice.

15. By accepting a co-insurance clause in your policy, you can get a substantial reduction in premiums. A co-insurance clause states that you must carry insurance equal to 80 percent or 90 percent of the value of the insured property. If you carry less than this, you cannot collect the full amount of your loss, even if the loss is small. The percent of your loss that you can collect will depend on the percent of the full value of the property you have had insured.

16. If your loss is caused by someone else's negligence, the insurer has the right to sue this negligent third party for the amount it has paid you under the policy. This is known as the insurer's right of subrogation. However, the insurer will usually waive this right upon request. For example, if you have leased your insured building to someone and have waived your right to recover from the tenant for any insured damages to your property, you should have your agent request the insurer to waive the subrogation clause in the fire policy on your leased building.

17. A building under construction can be insured for fire, lightning, extended coverage, vandalism, and malicious mischief.

LIABILITY INSURANCE

	No action needed	Look into this

1. Legal liability limits of $1 million are no longer considered high or unreasonable, even for a small business.
2. Most liability policies require you to notify the insurer immediately after any incident on your property that might cause a future claim. This holds true no matter how unimportant the incident may seem at the time it happens.
3. Most liability policies, in addition to bodily injuries, may now cover personal injuries (libel, slander, and so on) if these are specifically stated in the policy.
4. Under certain conditions, your business may be subject to damage claims, even from trespassers.
5. You may be legally liable for damages, even in cases where you used "reasonable care."
6. Even if the suit against you is false or fraudulent, the liability insurer pays court costs, legal fees, and interest on judgments in addition to the liability judgements themselves.
7. You can be liable for the acts of others under contracts you have signed with them. This liability is insurable.

AUTOMOBILE INSURANCE

	No action needed	Look into this

1. When an employee or a subcontractor uses his or her own car on your behalf, you can be legally liable even if you do not own a car or truck yourself.
2. Five or more automobiles or motorcycles under one ownership that are operated as a fleet for business purposes can generally be insured under a low-cost fleet policy against both material damage to the vehicles and liability to others for property damage or personal injury.
3. You can often get deductibles of almost any amount—say $250 or $500—and thereby reduce your premiums.
4. Automobile medical-payments insurance pays for medical claims, including your own, arising from automobile accidents, regardless of the question of negligence.
5. In most states, you must carry liability insurance or be prepared to provide other proof (such as a surety bond) of financial responsibility when you are involved in an accident.
6. You can purchase uninsured motorist protection to cover your own bodily-injury claims from someone who has no insurance.

WORKER'S COMPENSATION INSURANCE	No action needed	Look into this

1. Common law requires that an employer: (1) provide his or her employees a safe place to work, (2) hire competent fellow employees, (3) provide safe tools, and (4) warn employees of any existing dangers. _____ _____
2. If an employer fails to provide the above, he or she is liable for damage suits brought by an employee. _____ _____
3. State law determines the level or type of benefits payable under worker's compensation policies. _____ _____
4. Not all employees are covered by worker's compensation laws. Exceptions are determined by state law, and vary from state to state. _____ _____
5. In nearly all states, an employer is legally required to cover employees under worker's compensation. _____ _____
6. You can save money on worker's compensation insurance by seeing your employees are properly classified. _____ _____
7. Rates for worker's compensation insurance vary from 0.1 percent of the payroll for ''safe'' occupations to about 25 percent of the payroll for very hazardous occupations. _____ _____
8. Most employers in most states can reduce worker's compensation premium costs by reducing their accident rates below the average. _____ _____

DESIREABLE INSURANCE COVERAGE CHECKLIST

BUSINESS INTERRUPTION INSURANCE	No action needed	Look into this

1. Insurance can be purchased to cover fixed expenses that would continue if a fire (for example) shut down your business—such as salaries to key employees, taxes, interest, depreciation, and utilities—as well as the profits you would lose. _____ _____
2. Under properly written contingent business interruption insurance, you can also collect if fire or other peril closes the business of a supplier or customer, which interrupts your business. _____ _____
3. The business interruption policy provides payments to hasten the reopening of your business after a fire or other insured peril. _____ _____
4. You can get coverage for extra expenses if an insured peril, while not actually closing your business down, seriously disrupts it. _____ _____
5. You can get business interruption insurance to indemnify you if your operations are suspended because of failure or interruption of the supply of power, light, heat, gas, or water furnished by a public utility company. _____ _____

CRIME INSURANCE

<table>
<thead>
<tr><th>No action needed</th><th>Look into this</th></tr>
</thead>
</table>

1. Burglary insurance excludes such property as accounts, articles in showcase windows, and manuscripts.   _____ _____
2. Coverage is granted under burglary insurance only if there are visible marks of forced entry.   _____ _____
3. Burglary insurance can be written to cover (in addition to money) merchandise and damage.   _____ _____
4. Robbery insurance protects from loss of property, money, and securities by force, trickery, or threat of violence on or off your premises. _____ _____
5. A comprehensive crime policy, written just for small business owners, is available. In addition to burglary and robbery, it covers other types of loss by theft, destruction, and disappearance of money and securities, including thefts committed by employees.   _____ _____
6. If you are in a high-risk area and cannot get insurance through normal channels, you may be able to get help through the federal crime insurance plan. A State Insurance Commissioner can tell you where to get information.   _____ _____

GLASS INSURANCE

<table>
<thead>
<tr><th>No action needed</th><th>Look into this</th></tr>
</thead>
</table>

1. You can purchase special glass insurance that covers all risk to plate-glass windows, glass signs, glass brick, glass doors, showcases, countertops, and insulated glass panels.   _____ _____
2. The policy covers not only the glass, but also its lettering and ornamentation, if these are specifically insured, plus the costs of temporary plates or boarding up when necessary.   _____ _____
3. After the glass has been replaced, full coverage is continued without any additional premium for the period covered.   _____ _____

RENT INSURANCE

<table>
<thead>
<tr><th>No action needed</th><th>Look into this</th></tr>
</thead>
</table>

1. You can buy rent insurance that will pay your rent if the property you lease becomes unusable due to fire or other insured perils and if your lease calls for continued payments.   _____ _____
2. If you own property and lease it to others, you can insure against loss if the lease is canceled due to fire and you have to rent the property again at a reduced rental.   _____ _____

DISABILITY INSURANCE

No action needed	*Look into this*

1. Worker's compensation insurance pays an employee only for time lost due to work-related injuries and illnesses—not for time lost due to disabilities incurred off the job. But you can purchase, at a low premium, insurance to replace the lost income of workers who suffer short-term or long-term disability that is not related to their work.

——— ———

2. You can get coverage that provides employees with an income for life in case of permanent disability resulting from work-related accident or illness.

——— ———

GROUP LIFE INSURANCE

No action needed	*Look into this*

1. If you pay group insurance premiums and cover all employees up to $50,000, the cost to you is deductible for federal income tax purposes; yet the value of the benefit is not taxable income to your employees.

——— ———

2. Most insurers will provide group coverages at low rates, even for ten or fewer employees.

——— ———

3. If employees pay part of the cost of the group insurance, state laws require that 75 percent of them must elect coverage to qualify as group insurance.

——— ———

4. Group plans permit an employee leaving the company to convert group insurance coverage to a private plan, without a medical exam if that person does so within thirty days after leaving the job.

——— ———

GROUP HEALTH INSURANCE

No action needed	*Look into this*

1. Group health insurance costs much less than would individual contracts, and provides more generous benefits for the worker.

——— ———

2. If you pay the entire cost, individual employees cannot be dropped from a group plan unless the entire group policy is canceled.

——— ———

RETIREMENT INCOME

<table>
<tr><td>No action needed</td><td>Look into this</td></tr>
</table>

1. If you are self-employed, you can get an income tax deduction for funds used for retirement for you and your employees through plans of insurance or annuities approved for use under the Employees Retirement Income Security Act of 1974 (ERISA).

——— ———

2. Annuity contracts may provide for variable payments in the hope of giving the annuitants some protection against the effects of inflation. Whether fixed or variable, an annuity can provide retirement income that is guaranteed for life.

——— ———

KEY PERSON COVERAGE

<table>
<tr><td>No action needed</td><td>Look into this</td></tr>
</table>

1. One of the most serious setbacks that can come to a small company is the loss of a key person. But this person can be insured with life insurance and disability insurance owned by and payable to your company.

——— ———

2. Proceeds of a key-person coverage insurance policy, which accumulates as an asset of the business, can be borrowed against and the interest and dividends are not subject to income tax as long as the policy remains in force.

——— ———

3. The cash value of key-person coverage insurance, which accumulates as an asset of the business, can be borrowed against—and the interest and dividends are not subject to income tax as long as the policy remains in force.

——— ———

Source: *Insurance Checklist for Small Business,* Mark R. Green, Small Business Administration, in *Managing Your Small Business,* Robert T. Justis, Englewood Cliffs, NJ: Prentice-Hall, 1981, pp. 372-379.

STEP #6

Develop Forecasts and Budgets.

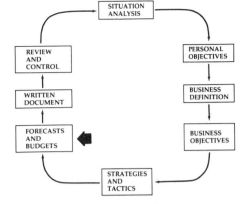

Having formulated an extensive list of tentative strategic and tactical decisions, the next step in the planning process is to forecast revenues (presumably sales), costs and expenses, profits, and cash. The process of preparing forecasts forces an entrepreneur to carefully consider the future financial position of the business. Doing so can minimize future surprises. Though initial forecasts for new businesses are rarely as accurate as entrepreneurs expect, the better the forecast, the more effective planning will be for the deployment of resources, the better customers can be served and the more profitable the business will be.

Sales Forecasting

Estimating future sales is critical since all other forecasts and budgets are directly or indirectly derived from the sales forecast. If the sales forecast is significantly off, there will be problems in estimating the requirements for manpower, equipment, raw materials, profits and cash.

To forecast sales, a combination for the following techniques should be considered:

- —*Industry norms*, based upon data for similar size and type business (often available from trade association data).

- —*Partner/investor opinion.* That is, ask key people who are helping start the business, then weigh their estimates versus yours.

- —*User's expectations.* If your business will only serve a few customers and you can identify them, ask for commitments and project needs based on estimates of what they expect to purchase.

- —*Competitor audits.* An entrepreneur opening a new restaurant might get some "feel" for demand by periodically visiting the competition at different times to see the level of activity.

- —*Simulated test markets.* Some enterprises conduct market tests in a small sampling of outlets to assess the sales potential of new products. Most small business entrepreneurs would find this process to be expensive and time consuming, but it could prove very worthwhile.

- —*Direct Mail sampling* to test lists is an economical way to predict response before undertaking the expense of a mass mailing.

DEVELOP FORECASTS AND BUDGETS (Continued)

Profitability forecasting.

Profits may be estimated after the sales forecast has been made and after costs and expenses identified. A worksheet such as the one shown on the facing page is handy for forecasting profits realized in a specific time *period,* such as a year. Of course, you should also itemize additional revenues and expenses particular to your individual business. The worksheet on page 72, for example, will help you identify start-up costs incurred before the business opens.

When computing profitability, it is sometimes enlightening to conduct a *sensitivity analysis.* In other words, consider a few alternative "what if...?" scenarios: What if sales (or costs, or expenses) are 10% (20%, 30%, etc.) above or below the estimate? A change in sales, costs, or expenses will not always have a proportionate corresponding effect on profitability.

On page 73 is an example of a balance sheet worksheet. This will be useful throughout the life of a business. A balance sheet provides an invaluable "snapshot" of the business' overall position at any *single point in time.* It effectively aggregates all of the profits, losses, assets, and debts realized in previous periods.

ESTIMATED PROJECTION AND FORECAST OF THREE YEARS EARNINGS

	Year: 19___	19___	19___
Gross Receipts	$ ___	$ ___	$ ___
Merchandise Cost	___	___	___
Gross Profit (Receipts less merch. cost)	___	___	___
Expenses			
Officer's Salaries (if corporation)	___	___	___
Employee Wages	___	___	___
Accounting & Legal Fees	___	___	___
Advertising	___	___	___
Rent	___	___	___
Depreciation	___	___	___
Supplies	___	___	___
Electricity	___	___	___
Telephone	___	___	___
Interest	___	___	___
Repairs	___	___	___
Taxes	___	___	___
Insurance	___	___	___
Bad Debts	___	___	___
**Miscellaneous (Postage, etc.)	___	___	___
Total Expenses	___	___	___
Net Profit (Gross profit less total expenses)	___	___	___
Less Income Taxes (if corporation)	___	___	___
Net Profit After Taxes	___	___	___
Less Withdrawals (i.e., loan payments, Proprietorship/Partnership)	___	___	___
Net Profit	___	___	___

**If sum is large, please itemize.

Source: Courtesy of the Small Business Administration.

START-UP COSTS

Money needed for owner or manager	$ _____	Until opening
Living Expenses:		
Moving expenses	_____	Once
Salary for owner or manager	_____	1-3 months
Land (buy or lease)	_____	1-3 months
Building	_____	Once
Building Expenses:		
Equipment	_____	Once
Fixtures	_____	Once
Decorating and remodeling	_____	Once
Salaries and wages	_____	1-3 months
Inventory	_____	1-3 months
Advertising	_____	3 months
Telephone	_____	1-3 months
Business Expenses:		
Utilities	_____	1-3 months
Insurance	_____	As required
Legal and professional fees	_____	1-3 months
Vehicles	_____	Once
Supplies	_____	1-3 months
Starting inventory	_____	Once
Utility deposits	_____	Once
Licenses	_____	Once
Advertising and promotion for opening	_____	Once
Cash Reserve (Petty Cash; Credit Accounts)	_____	1-3 months
Total Cash Required to Start a Business	$ _____	

Source: R.T. Justis, *Managing Your Small Business*, ©1981, p. 93. Reprinted by permission of Prentice-Hall, Inc., Englewood Cliffs, N.J.

BALANCE SHEET WORKSHEET

Current Balance Sheet

for

_____
(name of your company)

as of

_____
(date)

Assets
Current Assets

Cash	$	___
Accounts Receivable		___
Inventory		___

Fixed Assets

Land	$	___
Building		___
Equipment		___
Total		___
Less Depreciation		___
Total	$	___

Liabilities
Current Liabilities

Accounts Payable	$	___
Accrued Expenses		___
Short Term Loans		___

Fixed Liabilities

Long Term Loan	$	___
Mortgage		___

Net Worth $ ___

Total $ ___

Source: *Business Plan for Small Manufacturers*, Management Aid # 2.007, U.S. Small Business Administration, 1985.

FORECASTS AND BUDGETS (Continued)

Cash Forecasting and Budgeting.

Accurate cash flow projections are critical to the success of a new business. Just because a business is expected to be profitable doesn't mean enough cash will be on hand to pay creditors, employees, and taxes when the need arises. In fact, growing businesses often consume more cash than they generate. This is because increasingly large amounts of cash become tied up in inventory, equipment, facilities, payroll, and accounts receivable. Other entrepreneurs invest their entire savings to start a new business without a sufficient cushion of cash required to pay bills when due. In either case, it is useful to think in terms of monitoring and managing cash as well as profits. A worksheet such as the one shown on the facing page is useful for estimating cash flows.

If you are able to anticipate possible cash drains in advance of their occurrence, several steps may be taken to avoid cash crises. For example, to increase cash in the short term, you may be able to plan ways to:

1. Accelerate payments from your customers, e.g., offer discounts or other incentives to customers who pay early.

2. Grant credit to fewer customers.

3. Eliminate or postpone purchases from suppliers.

4. Negotiate extended payment terms with creditors.

5. Deplete inventories of raw materials and supplies before reordering.

6. Reorder raw materials and supplies in smaller quantities.

7. Arrange for a short-term line of credit from a local lending institution.

8. Sell long overdue accounts receivable to a collection agency.

HAPPINESS IS A POSITIVE CASH FLOW

ESTIMATED CASH FORECAST

	Jan	Feb	Mar	Apr	May	Jun	Etc.
(1) Cash in Bank (Start of Month)							
(2) Petty Cash (Start of Month)							
(3) Total Cash (add (1) and (2))							
(4) Expected Accounts Receivable							
(5) Other Money Expected							
(6) Total Receipts (add (4) and (5))							
(7) Total Cash and Receipts (add (3) and (6))							
(8) All Disbursements (for month)							
(9) Cash Balance at End of Month in Bank Account and Petty Cash (subtract (8) from (7))*							

*This balance is your starting cash balance for the next month.

Source: *Business Plan for Small Manufacturers*, Management Aid #2.007, U.S. Small Business Administration, 1985.

STEP #7

Write the
Business Plan.

By this time you have assembled hundreds of
answers and bits of information in response to
the seemingly endless onslaught of questions
raised thus far. As well organized as your notes
may now be and as clear as your thoughts are
today, at some point you'll need to recall precisely what planning decisions you
made, and why. If partners, employees, and potential investors are to play a
significant role in the business, they too will need to understand your plans.

So, this next-to-last step in the planning process involves the preparation of a
written document to organize and clarify your business plans. In fact, it may be
a good idea to write two plans—a detailed plan for yourself, and a shorter,
condensed version for others who may have no interest in the minute business
details.

Your plan should reflect the information you have gathered and the decisions you
have made throughout the planning process. The following two pages provide an
outline of a sample business plan.

SAMPLE BUSINESS PLAN OUTLINE

I. Summary

  A. Business description
     1. Name
     2. Location
     3. Product(s)
     4. Market and competition
     5. Management expertise
  B. Business definition, goals, and objectives
  C. Summary of financial needs and application of funds
  D. Earnings projections and potential return to investors

II. Market Analysis

  A. Description of total market
  B. Industry trends
  C. Target market
  D. Competition

III. Products or Services

  A. Description of product line
  B. Proprietary position: patents, copyrights, and legal and technical considerations
  C. Comparison to competitors' products, operations, facilities, quality

IV. Manufacturing Process (if applicable)

  A. Materials
  B. Source of supply
  C. Production methods

(Continued on next page)

SMALL BUSINESS PLAN OUTLINE (Continued)

V.   Marketing Strategy

    A. Overall strategy
    B. Pricing policy
    C. Method of selling, distributing, and servicing products

VI. Management Plan

    A. Form of business organization
    B. Board of directors composition
    C. Officers: organization chart and responsibilities
    D. Resumes of key personnel
    E. Staffing plan/number of employees
    F. Facilities plan/planned capital improvements
    G. Operating plan/schedule of upcoming work for next one to two years

VII. Financial Data

    A. Financial statements (five years to present)
    B. Five-year financial projections (first year by quarters: remaining years annually)
       1. Profit and loss statements
       2. Balance sheets
       3. Cash flow charts
       4. Capital expenditure estimates
    C. Explanation of projections
    D. Key business ratios

VIII. Other Pertinent Information, Plans

Source: Adapted from: ''Financing Small Business,'' *Bank of America Small Business Reporter,* October, 1980, p. 19.

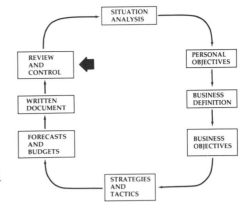

STEP #8

Review and Revise Your Business Plan.

A common occurrence is to carefully write a planning document, distribute copies to investors, obtain the required funding and then set the plan on a shelf to collect dust.

While there is value to thinking through the planning process and committing your thoughts to paper, the plan should be utilized as an ongoing reference document. Refer to the plan several times throughout the start-up process, then thoroughly review and revise the plan several months (and thereafter annually) after your business opens.

THE START-UP PERIOD

During the start-up process, focus upon:

- identifying the sequence of tasks that need to be done before the business can open,

- developing timetables for the completion of those tasks, and

- assigning yourself (or partners, employees, consultants, accountants, contractors, etc.) the responsibility of completing the tasks—though ultimately *all* responsibility is yours.

REVIEWING AND REVISING YOUR PLAN AFTER START-UP

When reviewing and revising the plan after the start-up:

- Don't be afraid to change your projections or assumptions if they appear unrealistic, or if conditions change.

- Modify your strategies or operating decisions if they are not as effective as originally envisioned.

- Try to maintain some degree of continuity. Avoid drastically ''shifting gears'' too often.

  Update your long-term plans every few months. Always have a vision of where you'd like the business to be in three to five years and what strategies will be required—currently and in the future—to move it in that direction.

- Keep doing your homework. You might have scouted the competition, conducted focus groups and rummaged through census data in the library before going into business, but much of the information gathered may soon be out of date.

REVIEW OF THE EIGHT STEP PLANNING PROCESS

STEP #1	**Conduct a Situation Analysis** • **Articulate Your Customer and Product** • **Evaluate A Location** • **Analyze Your Competition**
STEP #2	**Articulate Your Personal Objectives**
STEP #3	**Define The Business**
STEP #4	**Identify Your Business Objectives**
STEP #5	**Formulate Business Strategies and Tactics**
STEP #6	**Develop Forecasts and Budgets**
STEP #7	**Write The Business Plan**
STEP #8	**Review and Revise Your Business Plan**

PART THREE

SECURING THE CAPITAL YOU NEED

A few budding entrepreneurs are able to finance a business themselves. Most however will find it necessary to locate at least partial funding. Unfortunately, obtaining funds to start a new business is usually more difficult and more involved than obtaining a personal loan for a home improvement project or to purchase a new car.

To formulate a plan to secure the capital you need, address the following three key questions: (1) How much money is needed?, (2) What kind of money is needed?, (3) Where can the money be found?

How much money? There is considerable variation in the capital required to start a new business, so don't approach potential investors hoping that they'll know how much money you will need. In the fast food industry, for example, Kentucky Fried Chicken was originally started with an initial investment of only $105. More recently, McDonald's first restaurant in Moscow, Russia required a total investment estimated at $40 to $50 million! Start-up costs for most small businesses fall somewhere between these extremes—like a Subway sandwich franchise for $75,000, or a Western Sizzlin steakhouse franchise ranging from $744,000 to $1,454,000. The amount of money you'll need for your new business depends upon the type of business, the size and scope of your operations, the location and specific site you select, and perhaps most of all upon the particular business strategies you've selected.

SECURING THE CAPITAL YOU NEED
(Continued)

ESTIMATING START-UP COSTS

Fortunately, having collected the information for your business plan (steps 1-7), your determination of capital needed should be relatively easy. Refer to the "forecasts and budgets" section you will prepare for your business plan and retrieve the data used to prepare your estimated start-up costs and cash flow estimates. Consider the following suggestions:

- *Avoid padding your estimates.* Although some "contingency" expenses are understandable and expected, don't penalize yourself by being too conservative.

- *Don't make the mistake of raising just enough funds to open the business without sufficient funds to operate the business once opened.* Remember that cash is required to operate the business (especially as it grows). It may be months (or years) before the business is profitable.

- *Determine the funds needed at each stage in the life of your business.* For example, if you plan to initially purchase resale items from other manufacturers and not engage in manufacturing until the third year of operation, the initial funds needed won't require production facilities. Most investors (especially banks) will be more receptive to investing in stages as your business develops and proves itself rather than in a one-shot gamble.

WHAT KIND OF MONEY?

What kind of money? Rather than simply believing you need XX dollars for your new business, consider how the money will be used. This will help you determine the kind of money needed and the type of source to approach. According to John F.Murphy of the Small Business Administration there are four basic types of money. He explains:

- *Trade Credit.* This type of "money" is not borrowed. It is money you owe your suppliers who permit you to carry fast-moving inventory on open account. A good credit experience is proven evidence of your ability to repay borrowed funds.

- *Short-Term Credit.* Banks and other lenders often provide this type of money to carry your purchases of inventory for special reasons, such as buying inventory for the next selling season. Such loans are self-liquidating because they generate sales dollars. You repay short-term credit in less than a year.

- *Long Term Credit.* Such loans—for more than a year—are used for expansion or modernization of your business. These are repaid out of accumulated profits. Usually, the evidence of this type of loan in a small business is a mortgage or a promissory note with terms.

- *Equity Funds.* This type of money is never repaid. You get it by relinquishing a part of your profits to an investor. That is you sell an interest in your business.

For example, suppose you determine your *total* cash needs for year #1 to be $100,000, of which $70,000 will cover initial start-up costs for construction, equipment, etc., and the remaining $30,000 to finance inventory, accounts receivables and periodic fluctuations in cash flow. You might approach venture capitalists and long-term investors or creditors for the $70,000, try to establish a short-term line of credit with a local bank for $20,000, and negotiate extended trade credit with suppliers for the remaining $10,000.

WHERE CAN THE MONEY BE FOUND?

Methods to raise funds and potential sources of funds are limited only by the entrepreneur's imagination. A check list of potential sources is shown on the next page.

However, although you've done your homework and prepared a professional proposal, you should still be prepared to contact more than one source, because you may face some initial rejection. This is especially true when the economy turns sour. During the 1990-91 recession, for example, venture-capital funding for small firms dropped 66%. About 91% of surveyed small businesses felt a credit crunch according to National Small Business United, and 55% who applied were denied loans for business expansion or development.

Here are a few considerations regarding some of the more commonly used sources:

- *Banks.* Your banker may gladly loan you money for a new car or house, but be reluctant to do so for your new business. So, it is up to you to convince your banker that you've done your homework and are committed to the new venture. A copy of a thoughtful, carefully prepared business plan should help. Be especially alert to answer the following questions:

  —How will the money be used?
  —How will the money be repaid?
  —What sort of collateral will back the loan?
  —Are you trustworthy?
  —Do you have the experience and background necessary for your type of business? What about your management staff and key employees?
  —What are the long term prospects for the business?

POTENTIAL SOURCES OF FUNDS

- Commercial banks.
- Commercial finance companies.
- Venture capitalists.
- Credit unions.
- Customers.
- Employees.
- Equipment manufacturers.
- Financial consultants, finders, advisors.
- Founders and industrial banks.
- Insurance companies.
- Investment bankers.
- Mutual savings banks.
- Pension funds.
- Private individual investors.
- Private investment partnerships.
- Relatives and friends.
- Savings and loan associations.
- Small Business Administration (SBA).
- Small Business Investment Companies (SBIC).
- State Business & Industrial Development Commissions (SBIDCs).
- Tax exempt foundations.
- Charitable foundations.
- Suppliers.
- Trust companies (bank trust departments).
- Veterans Administration (VA).
- Venture Capitalists (VC's) — see next page

Source: R.T. Justis, *Managing Your Small Business,* ©1981, p. 156. Reprinted by permission of Prentice-Hall, Inc., Englewood Cliffs, N.J.

- *Venture capitalists.* Venture capitalists (VCs) generally make equity investments in smaller businesses with high growth potential. Many specialize in certain industries, geographic regions, technologies, or investment sizes. $250,000 is often the minimum size considered. When approaching venture capitalists, keep the following points in mind:

  —A typical VC may receive thirty or more funding proposals or business plans per day, only 10 percent of which will be read. Of those read, only a few will be investigated further, and even fewer will be funded. Therefore...

  —Make sure your business plan is professional-looking, clearly and concisely written. Some VCs believe an initial proposal should not exceed twelve pages in length. Forty pages should be the absolute maximum. The facing page outlines the elements of a venture proposal.

  —Stress your capabilities and those of the management team. VCs often base their decisions on the fact they are investing in you as much or more as in your business.

  —Knowing the VC before she/he receives the proposal is a definite ''plus.'' Try to get an introduction through your lawyer, accountant or other contact.

  —Have a stock liquidation plan prepared so the VC will know how to exit from the investment in your business. Most VCs want to invest in ventures with high growth potential (say, 30 percent annually) and then be able to ''get out'' before the business matures.

  —Services such as the Venture Capital Network at the University of New Hampshire help link entrepreneurs with potential private investors and VCs.

ELEMENTS OF A VENTURE PROPOSAL

- *Purpose and Objectives:*—a summary of the what and why of the project.

- *Proposed Financing*—the amount of money you'll need from the beginning to the maturity of the project proposed, how the proceeds will be used, how you plan to structure the financing, and why the amount designated is required.

- *Marketing*—a description of the market segment you've got or plan to get, the competition, the characteristics of the market, and your plans (with costs) for getting or holding the market segment you're aiming at.

- *History of the Firm*—a summary of significant financial and organizational milestones, description of employees and employee relations, explanations of banking relationships, recounting of major services or products your firm has offered during its existence, and the like.

- *Description of the Product or Service*—a full description of the product (process) or service offered by the firm and the costs associated with it in detail.

- *Financial Statements*—both for the past few years and pro forma projections (balance sheets, income statements, and cash flows) for the next 3-5 years, showing the effect anticipated if the project is undertaken and if the financing is secured (This should include an analysis of key variables affecting financial performance, showing what could happen if the projected level of revenue is not attained).

- *Capitalization*—a list of shareholders, how much is invested to date, and in what form (equity/debt).

- *Biographical Sketches*—the work histories and qualifications of key owners/employees.

- *Principal Suppliers and Customers*

- *Problems Anticipated and Other Pertinent Information*—a candid discussion of any contingent liabilities, pending litigation, tax or patent difficulties, and any other contingencies that might affect the project you're proposing.

- *Advantages*—a discussion of what's special about your product, service, marketing plans or channels that gives your project unique leverage.

Source: *A Venture Capital Primer for Small Business,* Management Aid # 1.009, LaRue Tone Hosmer, U.S. Small Business Administration, 1987.

- *Governmental Agencies* (e.g. Small Business Administration). The S.B.A. and other government agencies make funds available to small businesses, but there are often strings attached. For example, you may not qualify if you are able to secure financing through a bank, or you may find the required periodic reporting to be too bothersome. Other key distinctions about government loans involve the political criteria sometimes used in the evaluation of loan applications. For example, Merrill and Sedgwick* maintain that your chances for obtaining a loan are enhanced if the request is a small one, if you or your partner is a female or minority, or if your business will be located in a depressed neighborhood. For more information about Small Business Administration loans, call the SBA answer desk at 1-800-368-5855.

Other funding possibilities abound. One inventor in Michigan raised capital from a group of investors when he agreed that if the business failed he would give them the rights to the technology he developed. Some funding possibilities are located abroad, e.g., there are at least 80 to 100 Japanese companies exploring investment opportunities in U.S. ventures.

Finally, you literally may be sitting on other financing alternatives. One small business owner from Chicago, for example, does what about half of all new entrepreneurs do. She uses eight credit cards with an aggregate charge limit of almost $25,000 to finance many of her company's day-to-day needs. Although the interest rates on credit cards can be relatively high, the cards may be a viable financing solution when other pools of funds are dry.

---

*Source: *The New Venture Handbook,* Ronald E. Merrill and Henry D. Sedgwick, American Management Association, 1987.

CONCLUDING COMMENTS

By now you've probably realized that the phrase "small business" is a misnomer. There is nothing *small* about the quantity of hard work, skill and time required to start a business and make it a success. And certainly you are convinced that there is nothing *small* about the laundry list of quesitons that must be addressed before starting a new venture. We hope this book has not discouraged you; rather our hope is that it has challenged you.

After you have successfully negotiated the obstacles to starting your business, the future awaits. Though optimistic, do not expect *small* challenges or *small* changes in the future. The world isn't as stable as it was yesterday, and will be even less so tomorrow. Operating a small business is likely to become more difficult in the future unless you have done your homework. Consumers will have more choices which means increased competition, but also opportunities to fill some niches.

If one is to survive in "small" business it is necessary to not only "work hard," but also "work smart". Winners will continuously re-evaluate the appropriateness of the business' objectives, strategies, and mode of operation. Change must be anticipated and plans adapted accordingly.

Once the plunge is taken, persistence is essential. The entrepreneur must read, listen and observe. Ideas and insights must be borrowed and time is required to research customers, competition, and the current outlook. A new business owner must not be afraid to pick up the phone and call for help, asking as many questions as necessary until the answers are found. Learning must be continuous. Most of all, an entrepreneur must enjoy what he or she is doing and fight until victory is achieved.

Is small business for you? That's the last question we'll ask, but the first you should answer.

Go get 'um!

THE BACK OF THE BOOK

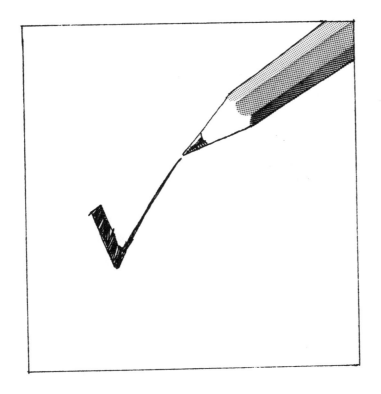

BUSINESS TERMS GLOSSARY

Accounts Receivable. Claims to cash on account which are expected to be paid within one year.

Agents. Middlemen that provide a risk-free procurement function by not taking title to the merchandise they buy or sell for their customers.

Amortize. Process of rationally and systematically allocating cost of an asset over the expected life of the asset.

Annual Percentage Rate. A credit arrangement term that applies to the relative cost of credit stated as an annual percentage, i.e. the annual cost of credit.

Assets. Probably future economic or income producing benefits of value that are owned or controlled by the business. *Current* assets are those that can be converted into cash within one year.

Balance Sheet. A statement of financial condition of the business that provides the owner with an estimate of the firm's worth on a given date.

Broker. An agent middleman or wholesaler who arranges title-free sales for his clients.

Buying Power Index (B.P.I.). A composite indicator of consumer demand in specific cities, counties, and metro areas. Published annually by *Sales and Marketing Management* magazine, the B.P.I. relfects disposable personal income, retail sales, and population in the area.

Capital. Account that represents real ownership and is the difference between the value of the assets and the liabilities. Includes owner's original investment, subsequent investments and profit derived from the business less losses incurred and withdrawals from the owner.

Carrying Costs. Expenses incurred from storage of inventory. Includes interest, insurance, taxes, deterioration, spoilage, obsolescence, handling and warehousing.

Cash Budget. An internal statement used by management to keep track of inflows and outflows of cash transactions over a period of time.

Cash Discount. Price reduction or discount on bills paid early. Terms of ''2/10, Net 30,'' for example, means that a 2% discount is granted if the bill is paid within 10 days. Otherwise, the entire amount is due within 30 days.

Collateral. Property that secures debt payment that the borrower pledges to the creditor. Collateral recovers all or part of a debt, if repayment of the loan is not forthcoming.

Cosigner. Any person that signs along with the maker of a loan or credit obligation, thus becoming responsible if the maker defaults.

BUSINESS TERMS GLOSSARY (Continued)

Cost of Goods Sold. Determined for the period by counting the merchandise left at the end of the period (physical inventory) and subtracting its cost from the total cost of merchandise available for sale.

Current Assets. Includes cash and other resources that can be converted into cash or used within the normal operations of a business within a relatively short period of time, usually less than one year.

Current Liabilities. Debts and other amounts owed to creditors by the business entity due within one year. Includes wages payable, accounts payable, dividends payable, taxes payable, and so forth.

Current Ratio. A commonly used method of measuring a firm's short term solvency by indicating its ability to pay current debts from current assets. Current ratio is calculated by dividing current assets by current liabilities.

Debt/Equity Ratio. A measure of long-term financial solvency of a firm showing the relationship between borrowed capital and owner's equity. Debt/Equity ratio is calculated by taking long-term debt and dividing it by Total Equity. A high ratio might indicate room for capital expansion.

Debt Financing. Financing through borrowing capital that must be repaid.

Discretionary Income. Disposable personal income less amount spent for necessities such as food, shelter, medical expenses, etc.

Disposable Personal Income. Individual ''after-tax'' income.

Double-Entry Bookkeeping. An accounting system where every debit made to one account has a corresponding credit made to another account.

Economic Order Quantity (EOQ). The most economical quantity to purchase, balancing ordering costs with carrying costs.

Economies of Scale. Efficiencies associated with larger-scale operations. For example, it might cost a manufacturer $100 to manufacture one unit, $180 for two units, $240 for three units, and so on, such that the average cost per unit decreases as production volume increases.

Entrepreneur. An individual who organizes and owns a business for the purpose of creating long-term wealth. The responsibility and risk associated with the business are also the entrepreneur's.

Equity Financing. Selling partial ownership in the business to raise capital.

Fixed Assets. Business assets such as buildings and equipment that will be used over a long period of time—usually one year or longer.

Fixed Costs. Fixed amounts that do not vary with changes in the volume of sales or production, i.e. rent, depreciation, interest payments.

Franchisee. Affiliated dealers for distribution of products, services or methods in franchising obtained by franchisor.

Franchising. Form of licensing by which the owner (franchisor) of a product, service of method obtains distribution through affiliated dealers (franchisees).

Franchisor. The business entity which provides the franchisee the right and license to sell a product or service and possibly to use the business system developed by the company.

Goodwill. An intangible asset that attaches to the successful operation of a business. Favorable factors such as location, product superiority, service reputation, and quality personnel often generate goodwill.

Gross Profit. Also known as gross margin, determined by subtracting cost of goods from net sales.

Inventory Control. The process of maintaining sufficient inventory measures to meet customer needs, weighed against the cost of carrying inventory to determine an appropriate inventory level.

Inventory Turnover (or Turn). Measures the movement of how rapidly inventory can be converted into cash within a period. Turn is calculated by dividing the cost of goods sold by an average inventory amount.

Liabilities. Debts and other amounts owed by the business to creditors.

Lien. A legal claim by a creditor on another's property as security for payment of a just debt. May also appear as the result of judgment.

Line of Credit. A revolving form of credit where a bank loans a business up to a specified amount as needed by the firm.

Liquidity. Ability of a business to meet its short-term financial obligations.

Long-Term Financing. Loans not to be repaid within one year.

Manufacturer. Business that produces goods for individuals and/or businesses.

Manufacturer's Representative. Middleman agent who markets related, but noncompeting products for several manufacturers or vendors.

Market. A specific group of people who have needs to satisfy and the ability to pay (purchasing power).

Market Potential. The maximum achievable combined sales volume for all sellers of a specific product during a specific time period, in a specific market.

Market Segmentation. The process of dividing a heterogeneous market into several homogeneous sub-markets.

BUSINESS TERMS GLOSSARY
(Continued)

Marketing Mix. The four sets of tools the entrepreneur may combine to shape market demand and facilitate transactions: Product, Price, Promotion, Distribution.

Marketing Research. The process of systematically gathering, analyzing and interpreting data pertaining to the company's market, customers and competitors, with the goal of improving marketing decisions.

Net Sales. Dollar sales amount remaining when reduced by sales tax and any returns or allowances.

Net Working Capital. The difference between current assets and current liabilities.

Occupational Safety and Health Act (OSHA) of 1970. Legislation that led to the government regulatory agency charged with the responsibility of creating, establishing, administering, and enforcing job safety and health standards in the workplace.

Operating Expenses. Expenses incurred directly with the sale of merchandise (selling expenses) and/or those expenses incurred in the general operation of a business (general or administrative expenses).

Organization. The sum total of the activities, processes, and people that define a business.

Organizational Chart. A graphic description of a firm which identifies key positions, personnel occupying those positions, and reporting relationships.

Production. The continuous process of converting raw materials into finished goods.

Prospecting. First step in the selling process, developing a list of potential customers who have a need for the product, resources to acquire the product, and the authority to purchase.

Purchasing. The business activity of securing goods or merchandise from an outside source.

Quality Control. Ensuring and effectively regulating the production of the number and type of goods manufactured to quality specifications.

Sales Forecast. Projection of estimation of sales, in dollars or physical units, for a given time period.

Secondary Data. Information that has already been assembled, having been collected for some other purpose. Sources include census reports, trade publications, and subscription services.

Service Corps of Retired Executives (SCORE). Consulting service composed of retired business executives that volunteer their management expertise to small businesses. S.C.O.R.E. chapters work with Small Business Institute programs in many colleges and universities.

Short-Term Financing. Repayment of loans within one year.

Small Business Administration (S.B.A.). A federal agency established in 1953 to assist prospective entrepreneurs in obtaining funds, and to preserve competitive enterprise in the economy.

Small Business Institute (S.B.I.). A cooperative venture between business colleges and the Small Business Administration that offers management assistance to small businesses.

Sole Proprietorship. Business entity owned and operated by one person.

Subchapter S Corporation. A form of business structure that limits each shareholder's liability (like a corporation), but profits and losses are reported by shareholders (like a partnership). Subchapter S corporations are limited to 25 or fewer shareholders.

Target Market. A specific group of customers at which a company aims its products and services.

Terms. The conditions or requirements set forth in a credit contract or agreement, such as a promissory note or installment contract.

Trade Discount. Reductions in price expressed as a percentage from list or catalog prices given to a certain class of buyers such as wholesalers or retailers.

Unsecured Loan. A loan obtained without pledging any security. That is, no collateral, no co-makers, no guarantors, etc. back the loan.

Variable Costs. Are variable expenses that vary directly with the changes in the volume of sales or production, e.g., raw material costs and sales commissions.

ADDITIONAL SOURCES

No single book, person, government document, agency, or organization has all the answers you will need to start your business. Consequently, a variety of sources should be consulted after you read this book. Contact your local library and your nearby Small Business Administration office (addresses for S.B.A. regional and district offices are included below). These sources will give you the most "bang for your buck."

If your local library has been designated as a "government depository" most of the census data and other government documents, statistics, reports, etc. you'll need will be available.

SMALL BUSINESS ADMINISTRATION

The S.B.A. will be able to answer specific questions about operating a business in your state. They'll also be able to provide you with a wealth of small business bibliographies, booklets, and pamphlets covering a wide range of relevant topics. Ask for their list of "Business Development Booklets, Form 115B," and their list of "Business Development Pamphlets, Form 115A". They may also be able to recommend new-business workshops which will be held in your area.

Here are some additional specific sources of information you might wish to investigate:

S.B.A. Regional Offices

60 Batterymarch Street, 10th Floor
Boston, MA 02110
(617) 223-3204

26 Federal Plaza, Room 29-118
New York, NY 10278
(212) 264-7772

231 Saint Asaphs Road, #640
Bala Cynwyd, PA 19004
(215) 596-5889

1375 Peachtree Street, N.E.
Atlanta, GA 30367
(404) 881-4999

219 South Dearborn Street, #838
Chicago, IL 60604
(312) 353-0359

S.B.A. District Offices (also consult the Yellow pages for a local or branch office near you)

150 Causeway Street, 10th Floor
Boston, MA 02114
(617) 223-3224

40 Western Avenue, #512
Augusta, ME 04330
(207) 622-8378

55 Pleasant Street, #211
Concord, NH 03301
(603) 224-4041

One Hartford Square West
Hartford, CT 06106
(203) 244-3600

87 State Street, #205
Montpelier, VT 05602
(802) 229-0538

40 Fountain Street
Providence, RI 02903
(401) 528-4580

Carlos Chardon Avenue, #691
Hato Rey, PR 00919
(809) 753-4002

970 Broad Street, #1635
Newark, NJ 07102
(201) 645-2434

100 South Clinton Street, #1071
Syracuse, NY 13260
(315) 423-5383

8600 LaSalle Road, #630
Towson, MD 21204
(301) 962-4392

109 North 3rd Street, # 320
Clarksburg, WV 26301
(304) 623-5631

960 Penn Avenue, 5th Floor
Pittsburgh, PA 15222
(412) 644-2780

400 North 8th Street, # 3015
Richmond, VA 23240
(804) 771-2617

1111 18th Street, N.W., 6th floor
Washington, D.C. 20417
(202) 634-4950

1720 Peachtree Road, N.W., 7th floor
Atlanta, GA 30309
(404) 881-4749

908 South 20th Street, # 200
Birmingham, AL 35256
(205) 254-1344

230 S. Tryon Street, # 700
Charlotte, NC 28202
(704) 371-6563

1835 Assembly Street, 3rd floor
Columbia, SC 29201
(803) 765-5376

100 West Capitol Street, # 322
Jackson, MS 39269
(601) 960-4378

400 West Bay Street, # 261
Jacksonville, FL 32202
(904) 791-3782

600 Federal Place, # 188
Louisville, KY 40202
(502) 582-5971

2222 Ponce de Leon Blvd., 5th floor
Miami, FL 33134
(305) 350-5521

404 James Robertson Parkway, # 1012
Nashville, TN 37219
(615) 251-5881

1240 East 9th Street, # 317
Cleveland, OH 44199
(216) 522-4170

85 Marconi Blvd.
Columbus, OH 43215
(614) 469-6860

477 Michigan Avenue, # 515
Detroit, MI 18006
(313) 226-7241

595 N. Pennsylvania Street, # 578
Indianapolis, IN 46209
(317) 269-7272

212 East Washington Avenue, # 213
Madison, WI 53703
(608) 264-5261

100 North 6th Street
Minneapolis, MN 55403
(612) 349-3550

Government Publications

U.S. Treasury Department
Internal Revenue Service
Washington, D.C. 20224

- Tax Guide for Small Business
  (Publication # 334)
- Tax Guide on Depreciation
  (Publication # 534)
- Employer's Tax Guide (Publication 15,
  circular E)
- Information Returns (Publication # 916)
- Tax Calendar and Check List
  (Publication # 509)

ADDITIONAL SOURCES
(Continued)

The Superintendent of Documents
U. S. Government Printing Office
Washington, D.C. 20402
(202) 783-3238

- Franchise Opportunities Handbook
- Census Catalog and Guide (published annually)
- Standards for General Industry (O.S.H.A. guidelines)
- U. S. Government Purchasing and Sales Directory

Useful Indices Commonly Found In Libraries

Standard Industrial Classification Manual
(Guide that provides unique number, i.e., SIC code, for each industry. Many other data sources are organized by SIC codes.)

Business Periodicals Index
(Index to information found in business periodicals and journals.)

Predicasts Funk and Scott Index of Corporations and Industries
(Index to information about goods, services, specific companies, and industries found in business periodicals and journals.)

American Statistics Index (A.S.I):
A Comprehensive Guide and Index to the Statistical Publications of the U. S. Government.
(Very comprehensive source, includes abstracts.)

Other Useful Library Sources

Statistical Abstract of the United States
(Contains brief statistical summaries from governmental and nongovernmental sources. Useful in preliminary stages of market or industry analyses).

County and City Data Book
(Includes useful market statistics for cities, counties, and states in the U. S.)

"State" Statistical Abstract
(Separate volume published for each state, covers seventeen categories of statistics within the state: e.g., employment and earnings, banking and finance, crime and public safety, vital statistics, etc.)

Survey of Buying Power
(Special issue of "Sales and Marketing Management" containing statistical data for cities, counties, and metropolitan areas in the U. S. Popular Buying Power Index is also included for each area.)

Census of Retail Trade
(Several census publications providing retail trade statistics for a number of industries and geographic areas)

Standard and Poors Register
(Provides useful data and descriptions of industries in the U. S., arranged by S.I.C. code.)

Annual Statement Studies, by Robert Morris Associates
(Useful financial ratio data for several types of businesses.)

Directories

Business Capital Sources
International Wealth Success
24 Canterbury Road
Rockville Center, NY 11570

Canadian Trade Directory, Fraser's
481 University Avenue
Toronto, Ontario
Canada M5WlA4

Co-ops, Voluntary Chains and Wholesale
   Grocers
425 Park Avenue
New York, NY 10022

Credit and Sales Reference Directory
222 Cedar Lane
Teaneck, NJ 07666

Department Stores
425 Park Avenue
New York, NY 10022

Direct Selling Companies/
   A Supplier's Guide
1730 M Street, NW
Washington, DC 20036

Distribution Services, Guide
Chilton Way
Radnor, PA 19089

Dun & Bradstreet Middle Market Directory
99 Church Street
New York, NY 10007

Dun & Bradstreet Million Dollar Directory
99 Church Street
New York, NY 10007

Food Brokers' Association,
   National Directory of Members
1916 M Street, NW
Washington, DC 20036

Food Service Distributors
425 Park Avenue
New York, NY 10022

General Merchandise, Variety and Junior
   Department Stores
425 Park Avenue
New York, NY 10022

Grocery Register, Thomas'
One Penn Plaza
New York, NY 10001

Mailing List Houses, Directory
P.O. Box 8503
Coral Springs, FL 33065

Major Mass Market Merchandisers
1140 Broadway
New York, NY 10001

Manufacturers & Agents National
   Association Directory of Members
Box 16878
Irvine, CA 92713

Manufacturers' Representatives, Directory
135 Addison Avenue
Elmhurst, IL 60126

Mail Order Business Directory
Box 8503
Coral Springs, FL 33065

Mass Retailing Merchandisers Buyers'
   Directory
222 West Avenue
Chicago, Il 60606

National Buyer's Guide
115 Second Avenue
Waltham, MA 02154

National Mailing List Houses
Box 15434
Ft. Worth, TX 76119

National Wholesale Druggists' Association
   Membership and Executive Directory
670 White Plains Road
Scarsdale, NY 10583

ADDITIONAL SOURCES
(Continued)

Non-Food Buyers, National Directory
1372 Peachtree Street, NE
Atlanta, GA 30309

Sources of Supply Buyers' Guide
P.O. Drawer 795
Park Ridge, IL 60068

Supermarket, Grocery & Convenience
  Store Chains
425 Park Avenue
New York, NY 10022

U. S. Government Purchasing and
  Sales Directory
U. S. Government Printing Office
Washington, 20402

Wholesalers and Manufacturers Directory
1514 Elmwood Avenue
Evanston, IL 60201

Trade & Professional Associations

American Entrepreneurs' Association
2311 Pontius Avenue
Los Angeles, CA 90064

American Federation of Small Business
407 South Dearborn Street
Chicago, IL 60605

American Management Association
135 West 50th Street
New York, NY 10020

American Marketing Association
250 South Wacker Drive
Chicago, IL 60606

American Retail Federation
1616 H Street, NW
Washington, DC 20006

Association of Collegiate Entrepreneurs
Campus Box 147
Wichita State University
Wichita, KS 67208

National Association of Retail Grocers
  of United States
P.O. Box 17208
Washington, DC 20041

National Association of Variety Stores
7646 West Devon Avenue
Chicago, IL 60631

National Consumer Finance Association
1000 Sixteenth Street, NW
Washington, DC 20036

National Federation of
  Independent Business
150 W. 20th Avenue
San Mateo, CA 94403

National Small Business Association
1604 K Street, N.W.
Washington, DC 20006

Small Business Foundation of America
20 Park Plaza
Boston, MA 02116

Smaller Manufacturers Council
339 Blvd. of the Allies
Pittsburgh, PA 15322

Periodicals

American Journal of Small Business
University of Baltimore, School
  of Business
Baltimore, MD 21201

Business Today
P.O. Box 10010
1720 Washington Blvd.
Ogden, UT 84409

Entrepreneur Magazine
2311 Pontius Avenue
Los Angeles, CA 90064

Dynamic Business
Smaller Manufacturers Council
339 Blvd. of the Allies
Pittsburgh, PA 15222

In Business: For the Independent,
  Innovative Individual
J.G. Press
P.O. Box 351
Emmaus, PA 18049

Inc., The Magazine for
  Growing Companies
38 Commercial Wharf
Boston, MA 02110

Income Opportunities
380 Lexington Avenue
New York, NY 10017

Journal of Business Venturing
Elsevier Science Publishing Company, Inc.
P.O. Box 1663, Grand Central Station
New York, NY 10163

Journal of Small Business Management
  International Council
  for Small Business
West Virginia University
Bureau of Business Research
Box 6025
Morgantown, WV 26506

Manage
2210 Arbor Boulevard
Dayton, OH 45439

New Business
P.O. Box 3312
Sarasota, FL 33578

Opportunity Magazine
6 N. Michigan Ave. Suite 1405
Chicago, IL 60602

S.A.M. Advanced Management Journal,
  Society for the Advancement
  of Management
135 West 50th
New York, NY 10020

Small Business Report
203 Calle Del Oaks
Monterey, CA 93940

Success Magazine
342 Madison Avenue
New York, NY 10173

Venture Magazine, Inc.
521 5th Avenue
New York, NY 10175

Books

Accounting Principles, by C.R. Niswonger
  and P.E. Fess
South-Western Publishing Company
Cincinnati, OH

Beacham's Marketing Reference
  (small business focus with annotated
  bibliographies for each
  marketing topic),
Walton Beacham, Richard T. Hise, and
  Hale N. Tongren, eds., 1986
Research Publishing
Washington, D.C.

Creating the Successful Business Plan
  For New Ventures,
by LaRue Hosmer and Roger Guiles
McGraw-Hill Book Company
P.O. Box 400
Hightstown, NJ 08520-9989

Effective Small Business Management,
  2nd ed.,
by N.M. Scarborough and T.W.
  Zimmerer, 1988
Merrill Publishing Company
Columbus, OH 43216

Encyclopedia of Business
  Information Sources,
6th edition, 1987 by Paul Wasserman, et al
Gale Research Company
Book Tower
Detroit, MI 48226

The Encyclopedia of Management,
  Carl Heyel, editor
Van Nostrand Reinhold Co.
450 W. 33rd Street
New York, NY 10001

Entrepreneurship: Creativity at Work
(collection of articles from *Harvard
  Business Review)*
Harvard Business Review
P.O. Box 866
Farmingdale, NY 11737-9966

ADDITIONAL SOURCES
(Continued)

Essentials of Managerial Finance,
by J.F. Weston and E.F. Brigham
The Dryden Press
Hinsdale, IL

Fundamentals of Marketing, 8th ed,.
by W.J. Stanton and Charles Futrell, 1987
McGraw-Hill Book Company
New York, NY

Guide to Consumer Markets (updated
   every 2 years)
The Conference Board
845 Third Avenue
New York, NY 10022

The Guide to Understanding Financial
   Statements,
by S.B. Costales
McGraw-Hill Book Company
P.O. Box 400
Hightstown, NJ 08520-9989

How to Incorporate: A Handbook for
   Entrepreneurs and Professionals,
by M.R. Diamond and J.L. Williams, 1987
John Wiley and Sons, Inc.
P.O. Box 6793
Somerset, NJ 08873-9977

How to Really Manage Inventories,
by Hal Mather
McGraw-Hill Book Company
P.O. Box 400
Hightstown, NJ 08520-9989

How to Run A Small Business, 5th ed.,
by J.K. Lasser Tax Institute
McGraw-Hill Book Company
P.O. Box 400
Hightstown, NJ 08520-9989

Information Bank for Entrepreneurs,
American Entrepreneurs Association
2311 Pontius Avenue
Los Angeles, CA 90064

Modern Retailing: Theory and
   Practice, 4th ed.,
by J.B. Mason and M.L. Mayer
Business Publications, Inc.
Plano, TX 75075

Planning and Financing Your
   New Business:
A Guide to Venture Capital
Technology Management
57 Kilvert Street
Warwick, RI 02886

Purchase and Sale of Small Businesses:
   Tax and Legal Aspects
by M.J. Lane
John Wiley and Sons, Inc.
605 3rd Avenue
New York, NY 10158

The Selection Of Retail Locations (classic),
Richard L. Nelson, 1958
F.W. Dodge Corporation
New York, NY

The Small Business Index (bibliography),
by Wayne D. Kryszak
Scarecrow Press, Inc.
52 Liberty Street
Metuchen, NJ 08840

Small Business Information Sources:
   An Annotated Bibliography,
by Joseph C. Schabacker, 1976
National Council for Small Business
   Management Development
University of Wisconsin Extension
929 North Sixth Street
Milwaukee, WI 53203

The Small Business Legal Advisor
by William A. Hancock
McGraw-Hill Book Company
P.O. Box 400
Hightstown, NJ 08520-9989

Small Business: Look Before You Leap;
   A Catalogue of Sources of Information
   To Help You Start and Manage Your
   Own Small Business
Louis Mucciolo, ed.
Arco Publishing Company
215 Park Avenue South
New York, NY 10003

Small Business Sourcebook, and Urban
  Business Profiles
Gale Research Company
Book Tower
Detroit, MI 48226

Strategic Planning for Smaller Businesses,
by David A. Curtis, 1983
Lexington Books
  (D.C. Heath and Company)
Lexington, MA

Venture Capital Handbook,
by David J. Gladstone, 1983
Reston Publishing Company

Who's Who In Venture Capital, 3rd ed.,
by A. David Silver, 1987
John Wiley and Sons, Inc.
P.O. Box 6793
Somerset, NJ 08873-9977

Miscellaneous Services

Bureau of Business Research
  (Location research)
200 CBA
The University of Nebraska
Lincoln, NE 68588-0409

Nielson Business Services
(commercial market research)
A.C. Nielson Company
Neilson Plaza
Northbrook, IL 60062

Reid Psychological Systems
  (paper and pencil honesty exams)
233 North Michigan Avenue
Chicago, IL 60601

William E. Wetzel, Jr
  (non-profit service to match
  entrepreneurs with potential
  individual investors)
Venture Capital Network, Inc.
P.O. Box 882
Durham, NH 03824

Yankelovich Skelly and White
  (commercial market research)
575 Madison Avenue
New York, NY 10022

NOTES

NOTES

NOTES

NOTES

NOTES

NOTES

OVER 150 BOOKS AND 35 VIDEOS AVAILABLE IN THE 50-MINUTE SERIES

We hope you enjoyed this book. If so, we have good news for you. This title is part of the best-selling *50-MINUTE*™ *Series* of books. All *Series* books are similar in size and identical in price. Many are supported with training videos.

To order *50-MINUTE* Books and Videos or request a free catalog, contact your local distributor or Crisp Publications, Inc., 1200 Hamilton Court, Menlo Park, CA 94025. Our toll-free number is (800) 442-7477.

50-Minute Series Books and Videos Subject Areas . . .

Management
Training
Human Resources
Customer Service and Sales Training
Communications
Small Business and Financial Planning
Creativity
Personal Development
Wellness
Adult Literacy and Learning
Career, Retirement and Life Planning

Other titles available from Crisp Publications in these categories

Crisp Computer Series
The Crisp Small Business & Entrepreneurship Series
Quick Read Series
Management
Personal Development
Retirement Planning